DO YOU FEEL AS OLD AS YOU ARE?

Conversations with My Granddaughter

Do you feel as old as you are?

Conversations with My Granddaughter

Anne Simpson

Illustrations by Todd Driscoll

HPA | HUFF PUBLISHING ASSOCIATES

Publisher: Huff Publishing Associates, LLC, Minneapolis
www.huffpublishing.com

Cover and interior design: Marti Naughton
Author photo: Jim Leslie

Scripture quotations are from THE HOLY BIBLE, NEW
INTERNATIONAL VERSION®, NIV® Copyright © 1973, 1978, 1984,
2011 by Biblica, Inc.® Used by permission. All rights reserved worldwide.

ISBN: 978-0-9908073-8-4

TO MY GRANDCHILDREN

CONTENTS

Foreword

These vignettes are not in chronological order, as the observant reader will soon discover. They were scribbled in my journal over a period of three to four years, with no plan to polish them for a book. But the subject of aging pushed itself farther and farther to the center of my attention, and it became more and more the focus of conversations with "old" friends. I realized that we vitally need to rub off the tarnish and talk about it.

Introduction

It happened suddenly though I had gone through all the preliminary
stages: empty nester, active community volunteer, grandmother.
I adapted to each in turn, and I was enjoying the new roles and
opportunities of middle age. I expected to be healthy and active far
into the future, so I was totally unprepared when suddenly fifty turned
to sixty and early retirement because my husband Bob was diagnosed
with Alzheimer's disease.

Sixty became sixty-five, and our world began to shrink. It grew
smaller, ever smaller, and then all at once I was seventy-five. That was
the year I became a widow. That year nature pushed me with pangs
and groaning into old age. I felt the ground shift under my feet. I began
to think of "the rest of my life" not in decades but in years and on a bad
day even less. Around me friends were getting sick and dying. I had
health issues of my own, and I felt my energy flag. Reality caught me
by surprise. As author William Saroyan said to the Associated Press
five days before he died, "Everybody has to die but I always believed
an exception might be made in my case."

The years grew shorter; they spun faster. Suddenly the subject
I once carefully avoided was at the front and center of my attention.
I talked about aging at family gatherings, with my contemporaries at
coffee shops and around kitchen tables, in church groups, and on walks

with my neighbors. Like the vignettes in this book, they were casual, meandering conversations yet had a serious purpose.

One day I asked my granddaughter if she ever thought about what it is like to grow old. Did she have any questions? To my surprise and delight, she did! Alison drew up a list of questions and her boyfriend, Ian, added more for a total of forty. (The questions are on page 3; the ones in italic became the titles for the chapters in this book.) I hope that their questions will provoke more questions, and that my observations and responses will encourage yours, so that we can have lively conversations between the generations.

I watched my parents and grandparents grow old, but I don't remember talking to any of them about what it was like. It is hard to believe in this era of Facebook and self-disclosure that an important topic such as aging was once taboo. But like politics, sex, religion, and money it was rude to bring it up, and elders felt ashamed to acknowledge their infirmities. Smile through the pain, put up a brave front, be strong, and at all costs, be polite.

Now thanks to boomers and millennials—our children and grandchildren—my generation is freed to be open about how we feel and who we are, both our state of health and our state of being. Now at last the end stages of life are being scrutinized as carefully as childhood, adolescence, and middle age.

Whatever the challenges, old age is a blessing, and I feel very privileged to have a part in this conversation.

Please join in!

Questions from Ali

Appearance

What is it like to find your first gray hair?

How does it feel when your skin starts to sag?

Do you notice that you're shrinking?

Is fashion limited when you get older?

Pop culture

What are your honest thoughts on current top fifty songs/hits?

How did you feel when gay marriage was legalized?

What are your thoughts on today's sexualization of males and females in the media? How does it compare to when you were growing up?

Do you see parallels between what was cool when you were young and what's cool today?

Emotions

Anything that you really regret or wish you did differently when you were younger?

How does it feel to watch your loved ones grow old or pass away (especially a spouse)?

How does it feel when your child gets married and starts their own family?

What are you the most worried about in terms of growing old?

What's it like to feel yourself getting weaker—physical and emotionally?

Do you view death differently now than you did when you were younger?

Anything on your bucket list that you haven't completed?

Do you get bored of life because you've been living it for so long?

What are your thoughts on modern technology?

Is it scary to live alone?

If you could live forever, would you?

What do you hope you can live to see?

Does age really bring wisdom?

Does growing old make you feel self-conscious?

Do you find that you're less materialistic now than when you were younger? If so, what do you value more now?

What do you miss the most about being young?

What's your favorite part about being older?

How did having grandkids affect how you felt about your age?

Funny (from Ali's special friend Ian)

Do you think there are limits to old-person hairstyles?

How is it watching all the old men get bald?

Do you ever act grumpy on purpose just so you can be the grumpy old person?

Can you tell if you have old person breath?

Is there anything you wish you would have waited to do until you were older?

Are you physically attracted to people your age?

What are your thoughts on "cougars"?

Do you find yourself making stereotypes about old people?

Do you feel as old as you actually are?

How do you feel when someone calls you "old"?

Are you offended by any of these questions?

Do you think going to school was worth it?

How do you want to be remembered?

What is the best food you've eaten in your lifetime?

Old Lady at the Y

She flails flabby arms, churning the water,
as her slack thighs march
to the rhythmic regimen of water aerobics.

She sweats.

While the spandexed bodies in yoga class
twist mightily into warriors,
she, with baggy sweat pants,
crouches into downward dog.

She grunts.

In the locker room—
breasts sagging, stomach protruding—
she sidles to the shower
between the tight abs and steel buns
of lithe young women who don't know yet
that goddesses must melt,

that the magnetic weight of nurturing life
pulls us down from sterile Olympus
closer and closer to the warm, moist earth.

She smiles.

1

Do you feel as old as you are?

A funny thing happened

It would never happen to me—the tennis player and skier, the tireless gardener and hiker, the lover of the outdoors—I would never become one of those little old ladies who shuffled gingerly along icy sidewalks. Nor would I, who was once called "Pretzel" in my exercise class, become a middle-aged matron walking the beach with thighs flapping below the billowing skirt of my bathing suit. I would always be lithe and golden tan, splashing in the summer surf.

I would not inherit the hearing problem that my grandmother refused to acknowledge when she sat at family gatherings, smiling and nodding, seeming not to notice how we shouted and strained to include her without being rude.

Growing old wouldn't happen to my friends either. We were firmly agreed upon that. Our generation was different. We stopped smoking, took up yoga, and ate our vegetables. We were so engaged with our families and community that we didn't have time to slow down.

But a funny thing happened on the way to seventy.

The stairs got steeper, and I started to use the railing—that is, if I used the stairs at all and didn't succumb to the temptation to take an elevator. Young people began to talk so fast that their words muddled. I strolled the beach leisurely, in long pants, a floppy hat, and sunscreen. Body parts needed replacement or repair. Friends died and I began counting my own time from the end.

I guess the surprise is that we are surprised to grow old. All our lives we are an integral part of the cycle of birth and death. When we are young, we lose pets or grandparents, meet people who are disabled by injuries and disease, or hear about soldiers who don't return from war. We tend gardens as they sprout and blossom and fade in season. And yet we try to remain detached about our own life cycle.

How do you know when you are old?

Bill says it's when you turn fifty and get your first mailing from AARP.

Deb says it's when you go out with your daughter and men ogle *her*.

Maybe it's when you look in the mirror and your parent looks back.

Ron says it's when the waiter at the restaurant or the cashier at the movie theatre applies the senior discount without even asking. "How do they know I am old enough?" Bob feels like the character in Wallace Stegner's novel *The Spectator Bird* who insists that he is not an old man—he's a young man with something the matter with him.

Pat says it's when you watch a young artist or hear an articulate young speaker and realize that their generation is in charge now. We will not change the world anymore, she says; we can relax, the future is in good hands.

Jack says it's when the clerk in the grocery store loads all the heavy items into one bag and then leans close to your ear, "NEED HELP WITH THAT?"

Leanne says it's when that clerk calls her "Dearie" or "Honey."

Maybe it's when you hold a toddler on your lap to show him the family scrapbook and he taps the photos to turn the page.

Maybe it's when you realize that you and your teenage grandchildren don't speak, like, the same awesome language . . . know what I mean?

Maybe it's when you are in a group of friends whom you consider your contemporaries, talking about the Second World War when you suddenly realize that none of them were alive at that defining time.

Maybe it's when you are with your book club, scheduling your next meeting, and you get out your little notebook and a pen. All the others consult their phones.

Maybe it's when you discover:

I have become a "little old lady in tennis shoes."

I have to use a step stool now to reach the second shelf in my kitchen cupboards.

I ask other shoppers in the grocery store to get items down for me.

I notice that legs of pants that fit last year are too long.

I notice that everywhere, in every crowd, people are so big!

Mirror, mirror on the wall

(How I wish that you would fall!)

It's a shock these days for me to look in the mirror, especially if I have been spending time with younger people—hard to avoid because there are more and more of them. I begin to think of myself as younger than I am, at least ten years younger, and closer to their age.

Recently I was at a retreat where I was (no surprise) the oldest participant, and I did a double take every time I went to the bathroom where there was a mirror over the sink. Combing my hair or putting on lipstick (now that's a generational giveaway), I couldn't avoid noticing the sun-damaged skin, the circles under my eyes, the chicken neck, and greying hair. I am still pretty agile mentally and physically so I can hold up my end of a conversation and keep up with a group hike, but I can't keep up appearances.

I wonder what would happen if our ideas of beauty could change as we age. What if the models for laxatives and Lipitor were not blond and buff but actually close to the age of the targeted consumer? Wrinkles might become a badge of honor, evidence of wisdom and valuable experience and not a cause for tucks or laser treatments. White hair might be accepted as more beautiful than colors that come in a box. I would like to think that beauty is a face kind and soft with a ready smile and eyes twinkling behind the trifocals, not a face that studies itself in the mirror, but one that beckons to the world. I don't want to be ashamed of looking my age.

So I'll fight the temptation to take a book to the beauty shop and hold it up in front of my face while my hair is cut or to keep my eyes on the floor when I enter a glass-walled lobby. When I shop for clothes I'll march bravely into dressing rooms with 3-D mirrors. Of course there are limits to our fashions and hairstyles, but limits make our decisions easier and save us time. My most cherished and limited commodity is time.

Keeping up appearances

Back in the day when I read *Vogue* and not *Arthritis Today*, it seemed very important to me to wear what was stylish and in fashion. First, I tried to fit in with my high school friends in their polo coats, skirts, and sweaters (buttoned down the back, of course, with one string of pearls). Later, it was little black dresses for winter, Lily shifts in the summer.

Fortunately as I grew older my style—if you could call it that— became more individual; the emphasis shifted from three-inch stilettos to flat shoes with good support. My skirts went down, necklines went up, sleeves were capped at the elbow, and I favored clothes that were comfortable. I wore slacks then learned to call them pants.

We moved around in our middle years, and along the way clothes bred in the captivity of my closet. Now it is crammed full to overflowing, and off-season storage boxes are tucked away in the guest room. I have faded jeans and sturdy boots from our time on the farm, and flannel shirts, long underwear, and down jackets from the North Shore. I spent years working in gardens and walking in the woods, but I live in the city now, in a condo three stories up—no yard, no garden, a few geraniums in summer pots. I would like to weed out my clothes as ruthlessly as I pared the garden tools from a machine shed full to a tote bag in my storage locker.

But here is the problem: these clothes still fit, and they are in good enough condition that I feel guilty if I keep them without wearing them and guilty if I give them away. My mother's theory was that if she hadn't worn something in a year, she was not likely to wear it again. She had no trouble giving nice clothes away. I'm sure they were appreciated and well used. My father, on the other hand, subscribed to the "you never know" theory. You never know when wide (or narrow) ties will come back, when skirts will go up (or down), etc, etc. I'm afraid I take after him. I store things till they are shabby, then hang my head and take them to Goodwill.

That long black skirt I bought seven years ago for a charity gala and the chiffon blouse to wear with it? I'm saving them . . . for *what* . . . another gala? I don't like big crowds and three-hour cocktail parties with silent auctions. I would rather send a contribution and stay home.

One Saturday after lunch at our favorite restaurant, my friend suggested that we walk down the street to look at a new store that had just opened. We were greeted by knock 'em dead displays of bright, splashy colors—short skirts, tank tops, see-through blouses. She said, "We don't belong here. They don't want us to spoil their image. They are probably wondering who these dowdy old women think they are."

I was wondering too. I was as uncomfortable as my friend—a familiar feeling in a clothing store. Over the loud rock music we tried to reassure each other. "Our money is as good as the young customers,' probably better. We have a right to shop wherever we want." Of course we do! But when we see clothes that would look really good on our daughters or granddaughters, it is not hard to conclude that we are in the wrong place. And here is the other problem: where is the right place? Who caters to older women who don't care about following the latest trend but want to look as attractive as they can and dress appropriately for their age?

Maybe I need to appreciate my overflowing closet after all. It saves me money and shame and grueling trips to the mall. I should take better care of those flannel shirts and chiffon blouses. "You never know . . . "

At the grocery store

Neon magazine headlines dazzle us to catch attention at the checkout counter:

New Slimming Techniques!

Makeup That Hides Your Flaws!

Facelift of the Future!

The model looks to be about fifteen. Is it any wonder that older women feel unattractive, redundant?

Even if she is slender, well-groomed, with flawless skin and perfectly behaved hair, how long can a woman maintain the ideal of feminine beauty? Gravity will win. Age will inevitably show.

We like to think that we look younger than we are (maybe we need to have our eyes examined!) and often feel better than we expected to feel at a given age, but seventy is not the new fifty. We are not the same in old age as we were in our middle years, and certainly we do not look or act the way we did in our twenties and thirties.

Advertisements and magazine articles tell a woman starting when she is very young that she is not enough. She must work hard to improve and maintain her looks—buy this eye shadow, take that herbal supplement, subscribe to *All the Time Fitness*.

A recent advertisement in *Parade* magazine describes the new Wonder Hormone: "Women everywhere have finally stopped pretending they're okay with growing old gracefully, and they are joining the ranks of the rich and famous in fighting like hell to hang on to their youth."

The other day I was looking through scrapbooks with my grandson. He pointed to my high school graduation picture. "Is that you, Grammy? You were pretty!" I wish I'd thought so at the time.

I wish all of us could be like my friend Jenny, who, when she was a child, spent a lot of time visiting her grandma in a nursing facility. When she came home one day her mother found her sitting in front of the full-length mirror, squeezing her forehead, pouting her lips. "What are you doing?" she asked. "I want to have wrinkles like those old people," Jen explained. "They are so beautiful!"

Follow through

My husband, Bob, loved to play golf. He was almost fifty-five when he
took it up. He wasn't very good at it, but he had more patience and
persistence than most people who have played for years. Even as his
mental abilities declined, he remained physically strong, took lessons,
studied golf magazines, and practiced and practiced. He liked to watch
the major golf tournaments too. We saw Tiger Woods win his first
Masters Tournament at nineteen, cheered for all the young upstarts,
and marveled at their youthful bodies stretching and twisting like
rubber bands.

I haven't played golf in years, but today, remembering Bob, I
turned on the final round of this year's Masters. There were the same
young whiz kids we followed all those years ago but now there was
more room between their pockets, maybe a bulge over the belt, and
their swings were shorter, stiffer. One of our favorite "boy wonders"
is called the Grey Fox. I suppose he plays on the senior circuit. I hear
myself cheering for him and the forty-three-year-old dark horse from
Argentina whose caddy is his son. I'm as partial to the underdog as I
ever was, but now the underdog is the older, not the younger player.

Funny how our idols age along with us—Shirley Temple to Maggie
Smith, John Kennedy to Jimmy Carter to Nelson Mandela, bra-burning
feminists to nuns on the bus. We need these contemporary icons, these
models of senior success—celebrity models perhaps, real-life mentors
for sure.

One of my mentors was Frances. At ninety-eight she was still
planting a garden. When I helped her she taught me more about
vegetables and flowers on the North Shore than I could ever have
learned from the county extension. She was an excellent cook and very
generous in sharing the delicious pies and cookies that came out of her
oven. Bob had a mysterious knack of stopping by on our garden days
just in time for coffee break. Frances loved to share her many gifts,
and she accepted her aging with grace.

When Frances needed home care and had to accept the indignity
of help in the bathroom, she reminded her very attentive son of all the

times she had wiped his bottom. "Now it's your turn." At the end of her life when she was in a nursing facility, her son brought her home for a dinner party. His wife made a very special feast, his sister and brother-in-law were there from out of town, and Bob and I were invited too. After we ate dinner, Frances grew tired and said she wanted to "go home." So her son and son-in-law picked her up to carry her to the car. Turning back to the rest of us as they went out the door, she waved and called over her shoulder, "I'm a two-man woman!"

There was a couple who had lived in my condo building and modeled successful aging for the rest of us. (They moved to senior housing when David was ninety-nine years old and Jean ninety-six.) Their concerned children who lived out of town had encouraged that move for years, but they "weren't ready yet." Today both of them still drive, play bridge both separately and together, work outside in the gardens at their cabin, and walk two miles every day—even if that means pacing the garage in stormy winter weather. They open their home easily and graciously. The shelves and the coffee table are full of books—long biographies of the presidents, histories, best-selling novels. They belong to book clubs and study clubs, and they are up-to-date on current events. David is a retired cardiologist and Jean a nurse, so they practice what they must have preached for years: physical exercise, mental stimulation, social and emotional connection, and a good diet (though David has been known to indulge in chocolate when Jean is not around).

And then there is Adele. She suffered a serious stroke when she was still in her fifties—a young widow who lived alone and couldn't get help for more than twenty-four hours after her stroke. She lost most of the use of her right hand and arm; she drags her leg, and she is bent over to half her height. Yet she still lives in the house where she raised her family, climbs up and down stairs to the bedroom and bathroom. She has adaptations to her car and a handicapped sticker so she can get out and about unless the roads and sidewalks are icy. And if she gets cabin fever in the winter she calls friends to invite them for lunch, cooking and entertaining so graciously that it is hard to realize how laborious that effort must be. Adele reads voraciously, loves to discuss ideas, and has a quick sense of humor and a sharp wit. She spends her summers in a rustic cabin on the river that has been in her family for four generations—four generations of strong, independent women, I would guess.

I still admire those young whippersnappers at the Masters with their natural talent and fresh hope and determination. I envy their energy and confidence. I will cheer for them all the way, and sometimes I will ache for them, too, because I know that they will go through some disheartening days ahead. We all do.

But older people are my models and mentors now. They have more history, more heft. I don't mean celebrities, just ordinary people living extraordinary lives, masters in the art of successful aging.

It takes patience, persistence, and humor. It requires practice . . . and practice . . . and it takes years to learn. Come to think of it, the driving range might not be a bad place to start.

Double standard

He doesn't notice his at first—a few grey hairs in his beard, at the temples. She sees hers immediately, plucks out the intruders, and keeps careful watch in the mirror.

As he ages he becomes "distinguished." According to current values, she "lets herself go." He blooms. She fades. It isn't fair!

"Have you ever noticed," my father teased, "how the male of the species is naturally brightly colored and handsome without any artificial embellishments?" He usually tendered this question when his three daughters were wheedling him for some extravagant necessity that would make us beautiful, popular, and cool—saddle shoes, a poodle skirt ("all my friends have one"), or foul-smelling permanents (he called them "temporaries") to curl our stick-straight hair.

There is a whole industry that feeds on women's fears of not looking good, of not belonging, beginning in adolescence and ballooning into old age. We must never leave home without eye shadow and mascara, foundation, blush, and concealer. We should trim our waistlines and tuck our wrinkles, lighten our teeth and darken our hair.

Men get up in the morning and shower and shave. Ten minutes flat and they are set for the day. But they are judged by what they *do* as harshly as women are judged by how they *look*, even in this enlightened age.

What if, in a radical shift, all of us could be accepted for who we are? What if we could really believe that beauty comes from inside and not from the cosmetics industry? What if a gentle manner, a sense of humor, and an ability to listen, compromise, and act responsibly were more important than our titles and our costumes?

Then maybe the first grey hairs would be as significant as our first steps, our first lost tooth, or early signs of puberty. They would signal that we are moving to a new stage in our life—a stage to be acknowledged and celebrated. We are on our way to becoming who we are.

Through the Woods

Walking through dark woods
we drop memories
like bread crumbs,
as if they could lead us back
to a past devoured.
We hold what we can
of love and grief,
slowly weave our way toward the clearing
where they will become one.
We rest to gulp
sweet pungent air;
we share the bread left over.

2

What are you most worried about in terms of growing old?

One phone call away

"One of the benefits of old age," he says, "is knowing how things work." Charlie has lived in a small town for thirty years. He was on the city council and was president of the Rotary Club; he still is very involved with environmental issues—an active mover and shaker in his community.

"You can make one phone call . . . " He understands the way his town works, what the issues are, and whom to talk to about a particular concern. He is widely known and respected, and his calls get through the system. "It seems like a small thing . . . " NO. It is not. It's about belonging. About feeling safe.

I remember having that feeling when we lived in a farming community and years later when we retired to the North Shore.

Many residents were natives; their families had lived in the area for generations, intermingled and intermarried. They knew more about the newcomers than we knew about ourselves, but we worked together, paid attention, learned to compromise, and got along. Help was always close at hand and personal.

I live in the heart of the city now. I don't know any but my most immediate neighbors. I can't make a direct call to a plumber or an electrician, a city official, or even a doctor. I push buttons, get put on hold, referred to another department, and put on hold again. If and when I finally get through, I schedule a doctor's appointment several weeks or even months ahead and reserve a four-hour window in the distant future for a faceless service provider.

I do know that I will have emergency help when I need it. Calling 911 is prompt and efficient. The nearest hospital is only blocks away, and in our small condo we look out for one another. Within weeks of moving in, I ended up in the hospital. The other residents (bless them!) noticed that my car had not been moved in three days and that newspapers were piling up, so with great concern and resourcefulness they tracked down the telephone number of my son, called him, and asked him if I was all right. I was grateful—so was he—and I am comforted still by their care for me at that time and when I came home. I have a safety net that allows me to stay in this place, but when I leave I always carry my cell phone, my wallet, identification, emergency contacts, medical and insurance cards, and a GPS.

This is quite different from living on the shore in Grand Marais! One day Bob "escaped" and wandered away from home in his Alzheimer's fog. While I was frantically searching for him on one side of town, a man approached him from the other side. He looked familiar. "Do you know me?" Bob asked the friendly stranger. He did. "Would you take me home?" He most certainly, most graciously would. Bob came safely back.

I have moved a lot in recent years, and I know that it takes a long time to feel at home. It starts with the small things like where to get a good haircut, have my car serviced, and find the nearest grocery store, the best doctor and medical clinic, the most welcoming and faithful church, and the most reasonable and reliable service providers. And by the way, whom do I call about the car-swallowing potholes on our street?

With every move I've started over, asking friends or acquaintances for advice, trying one person, one company, and then trying another. But I know that I will not live long enough to figure out how things "work" in St. Paul. I am glad to be here because I can reconnect with people and places I haven't seen in years, and best of all I am close to my children. I am lucky enough to be an active part of their lives, and I hope I will always be, but I do not want to become a burden.

I find myself thinking a lot about a continuing care facility. Groan . . . another move. But someone else would worry about how the system works, maintenance would be taken care of, transportation provided, and for monthly dues equal to a small country's national debt, health services would be available at the push of a button. My children would not have to be responsible, and I would be safe—but at what cost: premature dependency?

There is an apocryphal story about a woman who loved to travel.

She found out it was less expensive to cruise continuously than to pay for assisted living. She got all her meals, excellent medical care, stimulating and ever-changing table companions—her community was the ship. An interesting option. Hmm . . . I'd have to take bridge lessons I suppose . . . if only I didn't get seasick!

Charlie is a lifelong sailor, but I suspect that even he will want to put down anchor at the end of life. Will he stay in his familiar community or move to be near his children?

There are no right answers, no easy choices, no small things. Just BIG questions.

Timing is everything

I ask my son: When is the best time to trade in my seven-year-old car with 100,000 miles? Jim answers, "About an hour before you need major repairs."

When I am with my friends and contemporaries, we often ask each other: When, if ever, is the best time to move to a continuing care community? My answer might be "about an hour before I need the care!" Most of us feel that way, and we can laugh at ourselves because (have you noticed?) the universe does not seem to run on our timetable.

Of course we all want access to good health care when we need it. We don't want to give up our independence, but we don't want to be socially isolated if we live alone. We don't want to burden our children, but we want them to be nearby. The questions niggle.

Can we stay in the community where we belong or move to an unfamiliar location to be close to family? What are the options for care if we remain at home? What amenities does a care community offer? And—circling back to the beginning—when do we need to move?

Conventional wisdom says that we make this major move either when we are in crisis or before it is necessary. We are advised to be proactive, to choose the place we want to be. There may be a long waiting list, but if we are lucky we will have some choice in our apartment and the opportunity to sort our things and settle into community living while there is time to enjoy it.

I followed this advice about ten years ago. My husband had Alzheimer's, and I worried about who would care for him if I died first. He still lived at home, and we qualified for Independent Living as long as I was with him. So we moved from our rural home to a city a hundred miles away where there was a spanking new facility on a college campus that included adult day care and a dementia unit for him and three levels of care for me when the time came. It was closer to our family, met our health care needs, and provided the stimulation of events at the college and contact with wonderful students who helped me with Bob. We were twenty years younger than the average age in the facility, and I soon became identified as the gofer and the chauffeur. We very much enjoyed the companionship of other residents. It was perfect . . . we thought.

But four years later, I had to move Bob into the dementia unit. I thought it would be the worst day of my life but two weeks later the real nightmare began. He was kicked out! The so-called "dementia unit" was simply a locked ward in one wing of the nursing home. The staff rotated from other floors and had no specialized training. Bob was very agitated when he was moved there, and they couldn't handle him. Why couldn't they understand that he was terrified because he was in a strange place where people he couldn't see or understand were moving him, feeding him, and taking off his clothes?

We were forced to move another hundred miles to the Twin Cities where eventually we found a wonderful facility in the suburbs that specialized in dementia care. I moved into a condo in St. Paul, which was fifty miles away from Bob. I put a lot of miles on the car visiting him at least four days a week, but now I was living where we had started our life together, close to family and friends. When the dust settled, I realized that this arrangement was better for us than the one I had so carefully planned.

So now I am very resistant to planning. I know it is the most rational and practical and highly recommended procedure—at least for "other people!" I may be flirting with crisis by putting off a decision, but I prefer to think I am taking a calculated risk. I trust my children to find suitable housing should I be incapacitated, and I have learned that there is only so much advance planning that one can do. In time I may change my mind.

Meanwhile I have updated my health care directive and put my name on a waiting list for senior housing. But I will refuse the opportunity to move if my name comes up too soon, and I hope that when I leave my wonderful condo it is in a pine box.

Facing facts

My young friend Gail, who is in her early fifties, needs to understand
that I am an old lady. One day when she is visiting, I tell her that I will
soon be going to my sixtieth high school reunion.

"Hmm . . . " she puzzles, " If I do the math . . . "

"That's right." I say. "I am almost eighty years old."

Her eyes fill, she puts down her coffee mug, gets out of her chair,
and comes across the room to give me a long, loving hug. "I don't want
you to go! I don't know what I would do . . . " I tell her how grateful I
am to have known her. (That sounds a bit final, doesn't it—as if I am
saying good-bye.) But I am grateful! And more and more I am aware
that we elders never know when or if we will see our loved ones again.

When Gail was a newly minted minister, fresh out of seminary,
she and Bob were colleagues in her first church. He was her mentor
and she his valued associate. They worked together well. We came to
love her, and after a time we "adopted" each other. Bob ordained Gail,
performed the ceremony when she married Charles, and baptized
their daughter. In turn she ministered to him when he was disabled by
Alzheimer's, coming a long way to visit him, read scripture, and sing
familiar hymns. She officiated at the inurnment of his ashes. We have
chosen to be family for more than thirty years.

"I'm not going anywhere!" I tell her. "At least not yet." But I think it
is important that she realize I may not have much time left.

When elders are together, we often talk about our lives, about what
we have left unfinished, and what we need or want to accomplish
before we die. Reconcile with a child? Say good-bye to the people who
have been important in our lives and thank them? Forgive those who
hurt us and be forgiven by those we have hurt? Though there may be
many things we hope to do, it is seldom the unfinished jobs that rankle.
It is the broken relationships. We may have had a long and happy life,
yet we all need to come to terms with our imperfect selves.

I have only gratitude for Gail, and there is nothing I need to say at
present. She may need to talk to me, now or in the future, and I want
her to know that I will hold the space open for any conversation.

Asking for help

"Could you . . . ?" I venture as I struggle to shrug into my coat at the coffee shop.

"Of course!" the barista replies, smiling as she comes around the counter to help me.

"Please hold the door," I call to the man going out of the grocery store ahead of me. He does that—and more. He puts my bag in his cart and delivers it to the car where my neighbor is waiting.

I have my arm in a cast. I cannot drive for a week, and my neighbor offered to take me out to do errands. It was not easy to accept her help—after all, aren't I a modern, independent woman? But I really needed to get out, and it was so much more pleasant to go with her than in a taxi, so much more fun to treat us to flavored coffees than to pay for a fare.

I have been going to the Mayo Clinic for the last few months to get a definitive diagnosis and answers to my questions about arthritis. The other day I was scheduled for a biopsy of my thumb and warned that I couldn't drive myself home. So my son went with me to Rochester— a two-hour trip each way—picking me up at 4:30 a.m. to check in before the 8:00 procedure. It was very comforting to have Jim's presence there, and I am deeply grateful for the effort he made. After all, he has a job, a family, a very busy life!

Little did we know that the surgery, which sounded simple enough, would put me in a cast from the base of my fingers to the elbow. I can't use my right hand, and I can't lift my left arm because of the arthritic shoulder. I have to swallow my pride and ask other people to give me rides if I want to get out and about. I have to ask my condo neighbors for help with simple chores like turning the key in my door, zipping my jacket, and even watering plants.

I live in the land of Minnesota Nice, and I have been gratified to find out how willing people are to be helpful—strangers and friends alike. But I do not think this area of the country is unique. I talked to a friend in California the other day, explaining my situation to her. She drives friends to chemotherapy because she has been a breast cancer patient. "It makes me feel good!" she said. A friend in Virginia visits dementia patients to relieve the caregivers. A retired minister in Arizona volunteers for hospice. And they may not be called "hot dishes," but all over the world people bring food to families in distress. We are happy to bring, to go, and to do for others. Why, then, is it so hard to ask others to do a favor for us?

We are afraid to be a burden, to be dependent, useless. I told my pastor friend that I don't want to have someone take care of me. "Why not?" he asked, and I had to laugh. Both of us knew that Bob was a quintessential caregiver, and I would like nothing better in my current state than to have his help and his company. And the truth is that there are times for all of us when we feel weak and vulnerable, and we need special care—emotional, physical, even spiritual care.

I am trying to see this period as a "growth experience" and to learn from it for future reference. "It's only a week," the doctor said. Surely I can live with a cast for a week. But there are uncomfortable hints of weeks to come, and there are questions carefully tucked into the back of my mind that are pushing to the forefront now.

If or when I am permanently disabled, what services will I need? How can I get them?

Will I be able to stay in this home . . . to live by myself?

Who can I count on . . . am I willing to lean on my friends and family?

These are unsettling, ultimate questions. Henri Nouwen writes in *Our Greatest Gift: A Meditation on Dying and Caring,* "We ourselves experience dependence as uselessness and burdensome. We often feel discomfort, fatigue, confusion, disorientation and pain and it is hard to see any fruit coming from such vulnerability. Believing that our lives come to fulfillment in dependence requires a tremendous leap of faith."

It is becoming clear to me that I will not be able to stay in this home for the long run without some kind of outside help. It is not a question of whether I will become dependent but when, on what, and whom.

My cousin tells me I will be doing her a favor if I ask her to take me back to Mayo when I need to go. My friend in California says, "That's what we do at this age—we help each other!" I understand what they are saying—from the giving end at least—and I agree. After all I cut my teeth on "it is more blessed to give than to receive." But to believe that by refusing to ask for help I could deprive someone else of a blessing . . . now, that's a tremendous leap of faith!

ENJOY

Passing away

How do we know when it's over—a job, a relationship, a life stage . . . a
life? When something has been deeply, ultimately meaningful, how do
we let it go? I was a caregiver for eighteen years, and for a long time
after Bob died I wrestled with the questions: Who am I now? What
purpose does my life have without that role?

Looking back I see many other reluctant letting-goes. I went
through divorce. I moved from communities where I felt happy and
safe. I watched children and then grandchildren leave the nest. In
addition to Bob, I have said good-bye to family members and friends.

And yet I am always surprised by change—hurt by it, as if change
were an unfair personal assault on my carefully crafted plans. Just
when I get comfortable with one stage, it seems life moves me to
another. The older and less resilient I am, the faster changes come.

My "forever" friend moves out of town. I take Bob on a lovely winter
vacation to Hawaii, and by summer he is in the nursing home. One
day I am playing tennis, the next day I am having a hip replaced, and
the son I held in my arms just a few weeks ago is driving me to the
hospital with health care power of attorney. "It happened so suddenly!"
I exclaim to the doctor. He smiles and gently reminds me "your tires
have some tread on them."

I saved a column that Ellen Goodman wrote when she retired.
"There's a trick to the Graceful Exit," she begins. "It means leaving
what is over without denying its validity or its past importance in our
lives." She's right of course. But I am not very graceful. It is so hard
for me to leave what is over! Sometimes the only way I can move away
from something bright and beautiful is to paint it dark; sometimes I
part with someone by belittling our relationship.

I understand my friend who can't get over the loss of her daughter.
"I have to hold on to the pain," she says. "It's all I have left of her!" The
older we are, the more familiar we become with pain. We carry it in our
brittle bones. But experiences of love and growth and joy pulse through
us too, and we carry all of ourselves into the future. "Every exit line is
an entry," Goodman writes. Every ending becomes a new beginning.

Humble pie

In the past few years, I began to notice that my friends were slowing down, beginning to look older . . . hmm . . . but I chose to ignore my own symptoms of aging. Until I couldn't anymore.

The minor aches and pains of arthritis have become more serious. Suddenly my bones are being "eaten" by inflammation and nothing the doctors and I have tried so far is helping. I have constant pain. I can't raise my arms above my shoulders. I can't reach the second shelf in my kitchen cupboard. My hands are too weak to hold a filled dinner plate or open a jar or push a heavy door. Getting dressed is an Olympic event—turning somersaults to get my arm in a sleeve, twisting and bending to pull up my pants, then pacing myself for the marathon of zippers and buttons and snaps. Personal best time: more than an hour.

The other day I asked my son to drive me to the Mayo Clinic for a checkup. I wanted to have an extra pair of ears; I wanted him to ask the questions I hadn't considered. He is really insightful, good at both listening and articulating. It makes the trip much more pleasant for me to have his company, but it is no longer a luxury. Going alone is not an option in the winter, at least. It has become impossible for me to drive when the roads are packed with heavy snow. I simply can't turn the wheel far enough to stay out of the way of other cars when we meet on narrowed streets. I can't get into tight parking spaces. I don't trust myself to control the car if it should skid. And so I have come to the stage I most dreaded: the time when I will become a burden to my family and to others. I've reached the end of Independence Road.

But I'm not ready to give up! I still have dreams. There are places I want to go—trips I couldn't take when I was a caregiver. There are projects to do, work to contribute, invitations to accept, people to love, and a beautiful world to enjoy.

But, but . . . I do not want to be a nuisance, to stand in anyone's way, to slow others down. I will have to make accommodations: adapt, change some lifelong habits, let go of expectations, constantly sort and evaluate. I'm sure that one of the hardest things I will have to learn is to ask for help. Who knew that old age would be such an active, challenging time?

Pride has served me well in the past, my son reminds me. "But now is the time to learn a little humility." (How did this kid get so smart?)

I won't . . . I will.

I want . . . I can't.

Thank you . . . thank you.

Worry birds

Chinese proverb: That the birds of worry and care fly over your head—this you cannot help. But that they build nests in your hair—*this* you can prevent.

"I didn't think to worry about this!" Ellie exclaimed. "My mother had cancer, my sister had cancer, and there is heart disease on my father's side. It didn't occur to me that I could get macular degeneration."

My mother-in-law had a big family. She took it upon herself to worry about each and every one—her daughter with Parkinson's, her son in the military, the oldest grandchildren learning to drive, and the newest, tiniest babies. If something happened that she hadn't worried about, it was all her fault! It was a big job being responsible for so many people scattered around the globe, not to mention their family pets, friends, and significant others.

I too have nests in my hair. At the least provocation, I jump immediately to the "worst case scenario." If I have a bad cold, I'm sure it is double pneumonia. Arthritic joints and stiffness? I must be ready for Assisted Living. I even picture my final days with the family weeping at my bedside as I comfort and release them. My vision is 3-D, technicolor, and surround sound. But soon enough the lights come up, and thanks to the miracles of modern science I can take a pill or go to physical therapy and get on with my life.

It would be a tad less dramatic to "consider the lilies." Pat is a clergywoman who had serious surgery a few months ago. A kidney was removed and she knows that her cancer probably will come back.

"I can't do a thing about it now," she says. "I'll worry when there is something to worry about," and she reminds me of the lilies in the field. Meanwhile she will scrupulously follow doctor's orders, go for checkups as scheduled, and next year she will move to Atlanta to spare her daughter long-distance caregiving.

Once in awhile I have dark, sleepless nights that arrive out of nowhere. Worries come and come, pouring into each other, and I am powerless to dam the flood of negative thoughts with deep breathing, positive affirmation, or prayer. Sometimes they are petty and disappear with the dawn, but other times worries that I keep carefully hidden in the daytime rise to the surface at night: I don't want to be burden. I am afraid of being abandoned.

I wish I could be as objective as Dennis, my CEO friend, who says that he is genetically indisposed to worry. If there is a problem, he will fix it—if it can't be fixed, he'll let it go. Or that I could keep things in perspective like Jane, a Brit, who stays calm, carries on, and jollies others along the way as she copes impeccably with any family upset.

When my aunt was diagnosed with end-stage breast cancer, she sighed, "Well, at least I know how I will die." She seemed almost relieved—there was one less thing to worry about. She would have time to tidy up some loose ends.

Some people browse through a book and look at the end before they read it; that drives me crazy! But we all want to know how the story ends, don't we? We dwell in mystery and yet we seek certainty—we try to control our dwindling lives.

If you want to make God laugh, the saying goes, tell her your plans.

And don't forget to mention your worries.

Those moments

They come unbidden, unwelcome—waking us from a sound sleep or
a vivid dream in the dark of night, winding between the lines of an
article we are reading about health care or end of life, whispering to us
when we visit an elderly friend.

I am going to die.

What will it be like?

Am I ready?

What have I left undone?

In these moments, intimations of our own death come as a
revelation, as if we alone among all God's creatures might be immortal.
What were we thinking?

In the light of day we prepare for our ending. We write our wills and
health care directives; we talk to friends and family about what we want;
we consider the options rationally. Organizing and planning, we hold
off the terror. But when our defenses are down these moments come to
remind us that we are not in control. We never have been; we cannot be.

There are reminders all along the way of course, but we choose to
ignore them: the serious illness, the loss of a friend, the tragic accident
in our community. We grieve, then all too quickly we move on.

How do we live with the painful recognition that life is short, that
we will never be able do all that we would like to do, that the world
will keep spinning without us? My cousin says that as she ages she
is constantly reinventing herself. We can imagine a new and different
self, but we can't imagine our nonexistence.

We want to believe there will be time—time to recapture the hours
we have wasted, make amends to people we love, contribute something
lasting to those we leave behind. But in our most vulnerable moments
we know that time is running out and we are afraid.

Is it possible that we need this fear to remind us that there are
moments of joy and love and beauty? Moments of grace when we are at
peace with the world in spite of ourselves? We cannot know when they
will come, or how or where, and sometimes they appear unbidden but
welcome, in the most ordinary times and places—sitting by the lake on

a quiet Sunday afternoon or watching the sunset with a beloved friend or breaking bread with the family.

In her poem "Sometimes" Mary Oliver reminds us to pay attention. I agree. Pay attention to both the joy and the pain so that even in dark moments, we might be astonished.

B-o-r-i-n-g

When I was younger I thought old people who talked about their aches and pains were boring. And so they were . . . so now am I. Our children do not want to know about aging, and they don't want the valued elders in their lives to change, so we conspire with them to keep alive the myth that we can have what we all want: healthy, productive, pain-free lives, forever and ever, amen.

But since this is not a perfect world, and we don't always get what we want (hard as we try), we have to make a choice. On cold, grey winter mornings I am tempted to pull the covers over my head, curl into a fetal position, and sleep the day away; like other primates we are genetically programmed to withdraw to a safe place, lick our wounds, and concentrate on caring for ourselves.

But there is another, better way—though it may require some painful reflection.

What do I most value in my life?

Whom do I love?

How can I contribute?

What do I feel called to do . . . and how can I do it?

What accommodations need to be made?

An elderly friend says you have to be strong to grow old. Yes. And brave. And not boring, and though it may hurt every step of the way, (shhhhh) we must not tell the children.

Bragging or complaining

A friend has an elderly mother who complains to her about very specific problems with her left eye. It hurts, it waters constantly, it gets so tired that she can't read; there is a spot in the middle where she can't focus. Alarmed, the daughter takes her to an eye doctor. But now the mother becomes vague and tentative. "Well, you know . . . I have a little trouble . . . nothing serious . . . it's probably old age . . . I shouldn't complain . . . I don't expect you can do anything."

A man I know who has neuropathy in both legs goes to a gala fundraising event for the nonprofit to which he is very committed. The cocktail hour and silent auction before dinner seem interminable. For two hours he stands on the concrete floor of a refurbished train depot, knowing that he will have a restless night and acute pain tomorrow. Would he join other senior citizens seated on the travelers' benches against the wall? "Of course not!"

We are embarrassed to be old. Ashamed . . . as if we have done something wrong to live such a long life. We even may lie about our age. We fear that we will be a burden on society, a nuisance to the children, taking up space and consuming resources, contributing nothing to the youthful culture we inhabit. We forget things and our gait becomes shuffling and slow, but still we pretend that aging won't happen to us. We dye our hair and medicate aches and pains, go for walks, watch our diet, and hide "glitches" from our friends and family so no one will take away our driver's license.

I hear it everywhere and all the time:

I'm soooo sorry.

Please don't bother about me.

I don't want to interfere.

Will Rogers said, "Eventually you will reach a point when you stop lying about your age and start bragging about it." I would like to live in a world where we do start bragging! Eventually . . . Why not now?

Pain in the neck

Is this what old age means? Is pain the best kept secret of our active elders? If so, it is one that my parents' and grandparents' generation didn't share with us.

I didn't expect this! Of course I didn't "expect" to grow old either. Even if I lived to a ripe old age, I planned to be healthy and totally engaged until the very end. I thought pain had been "cured" in the twenty-first century. Just watch the evening news: there is a pill to pop for heart disease, cancer, arthritis, diabetes, and even ED (and if a four-hour erection is an inconvenient side effect . . . well, the guarantee of lifelong sexual activity makes it all worthwhile). There is a cure for drooping eyelids, sagging chin, flabby abs, and depression. There are even potions and patches to delay the onset of Alzheimer's. Quack claims—and I believed them all!

Never did I realize until this year how debilitating, how restricting, how life changing pain can be. I'm not a stranger to pain, after all. I've delivered three children, had five major surgeries in my lifetime, and accumulated my share of cuts and bruises along the way. But never before have I experienced chronic pain. Always I would get better. With bed rest or physical therapy or whatever the doctor ordered, in time I would be good as new.

Now I wake up in the morning convinced for a few short moments that I am young and strong again, that the day ahead of me will be pain free. But as soon as I turn over or try to hop out of bed, I remember that I don't hop any more. My shoulder, neck, and hands are so riddled with arthritis that I am slow and stiff and clumsy. The daily activities that I once did without thinking are giant chores: dressing, showering, cooking simple meals that I can't taste in pots that I can barely lift.

I want to tell somebody! I want to cry and whine and be comforted, kissed and made "all well." But the beloved man who would have cared for me needed care himself as he suffered the mental pain of Alzheimer's. No one can understand this dilemma except other elders who have their own health issues—and so begins the organ recital, musical background for far too many conversations.

Senior Moments

Like clouds snagged in bare branches,
words pause, then drift away,
dislodged by the slightest breeze

and I search the open sky
for those wisps of wisdom
that were tipping my tongue just moments ago,

but they have evaporated into the atmosphere
only to return
in a sudden shower

watering my parched brain
sometime
when I least expect it.

3

What's it like to feel yourself getting weaker— physically and emotionally?

I dunno

How is your week going? What are your plans? What have you been up to?

These questions come up all the time in casual conversations with my family or friends, and I appreciate their interest but I am stumped, even irritated, by the questions because I can't remember! My mind freezes and without looking at my calendar I can't think of a single interesting thing that I have been doing, even when I know that I have been busy and I've had many invigorating days. When I answer the questions, I sound like a teenager. "Nothin' . . . I dunno . . . "

What have you been reading lately?

"Well, umm . . ." I can picture the book . . . it has a blue cover with red print and it is on the coffee table. Oh, yes! Suddenly it comes to me and when it does, I can usually think back to other recent readings and we can have a conversation. But something like an ice floe blocks the stream of consciousness. I suppose it is fear—fear that I will look stupid, or even worse, sound old.

What is the name of_____?

A friend has taught me to parry that question with another: How soon do you need to know?

These moments are to be expected. I know that. They are not worrisome—yet. But I get impatient with myself nonetheless and embarrassed because my life is full. It is as busy as I want it to be with interesting people and exciting projects, and yet when I mentally dismiss my activities and connections it must appear boring. I am not a boring person, but I sound as dull as I thought my elders were when I was young. Now, of course, I realize how wrong I was!

My schedule has changed as I have grown older. I spend more time on medical appointments and health maintenance and the activities of daily living, less time with committees and carpools. I relish quiet hours with friends over lunch or at a movie, and I avoid huge crowds. I keep up with my household chores and volunteer in the community and at church. I am learning to enjoy solitude. I read a lot and I write. I think that as we age we become outwardly less involved and inwardly more active. We are trying to figure out who we are and what our life has meant, and we have a lot of work to do!

I went on a walk with my neighbor the other day. She is a brilliant woman who just earned her PhD with distinction at the age of seventy.

"So . . ." I asked, as we trekked along. "What have you been doing since graduation? What will you do now?"

A long pause. "I dunno."

Take a hike

"I just don't want to do this any more," she sighed into the telephone. "I've lost the fire for it!" My friend lives in California. She belongs to a hiking group of twenty women who have been together for years, meeting for long walks on Monday, Wednesday, and Friday. Every year they take a week away for a serious hike—strenuous, fast-paced, rugged terrain. They train for months ahead of time. This year they are going to Zion National Park.

But Charlotte is packing a measure of reluctance along with sunscreen and her windbreaker, boots, and walking stick. She enjoys all these women and loves being a part of their group, but she has developed heart issues that slow her down. She doesn't want to hold the others back or disappoint her friends, and she knows that she cannot keep up with them as she did in days past when they all relished testing their strength and endurance.

For one week this congenial group will take time out of their busy schedules to live and hike in a spectacular setting. They will cook simple meals together, stay in a cabin that is rustic but spacious and comfortable. The forecast is for ideal weather. What's not to like? Of course she wants to go! "But . . . but I want to enjoy it," Charlotte says. "I want to walk slowly, look around to really see, stop once in awhile, and just sit . . . "

Will she inconvenience or annoy the others if she slows her pace— or more worrisome—will she endanger herself if she does not?

It is time for her hiking group to have THE TALK. The talk that my book group had a few years ago. One of the younger women gently raised the issue of aging. We need to be considerate of each other, she said, and patient when one of us forgets a meeting or arrives too late or doesn't get the reading done. Naturally she was referring to the other, older members, but as it happened, she herself forgot the next meeting—and she was hostess!

Charlotte has talked to her friends and explained her health situation. She may have to do it again . . . and again. But since most of the women are in their seventies, she is certain to find others who have similar concerns. They may even vie for the chance to stay back with her and spend a day leisurely walking or reading on the porch. The group may thank her. By sharing her truth, she frees them all.

These women have a responsibility to each other and have guidelines they follow for comfort and safety—they are bonded more by mutual interests and affection than by rules. Charlotte can do almost anything she wants to do—or must do—without feeling guilty. That is the good news about old age. She can hike or sit, take a nap or read, and if she doesn't like her book, she has earned the right not to finish it. So have they all. By taking care of herself, Charlotte brings health to the group.

Slowing down is a gift that age offers us. The gift of sauntering in the huge panoramic landscape . . . the gift of studying tiny spring blossoms that appear in the desert overnight . . . the gift of leaning back against a warm rock and listening to birds or the skittering animal sounds . . . the gift of casual conversation . . . the memories and deep connections that will sustain both individuals and a group into the future.

Traveling mercies, Char! And hey, next year can I come too?

Matinees

"Note to self," says Trish: "Matinees!"

It is dark, well below zero; the roads are icy and holiday traffic is heavy. We have each driven half an hour to meet for supper before a Christmas concert and are realizing, fighting the realization, that it is no longer comfortable or even safe to do this. We are vulnerable.

What if we have car trouble on the freeway?

What if we get lost?

I have a poor sense of direction in broad daylight and whether she would admit it or not, so does Trish.

I know I don't see as well at night as I used to, and my reactions are slower—so far I'm sure they are not dangerously slow. But I am afraid of young drivers who speed recklessly, too fast for the conditions, while my son worries about old people who are pokey and tentative.

The time will come when I have to give up my license. I admire those seniors who do it voluntarily as Bob did, saying, "I don't want to hurt somebody." I hope I can be so gracious because there are too many horror stories of old people who will not heed family or doctors or anybody else, who will not give up driving even when they are a menace on the road.

We want to maintain our independence.

Hitching rides is embarrassing.

Public transportation is inconvenient.

Taxis are expensive.

Oh, we have our reasons—good reasons!

But here is another "growth opportunity," Trish reminds me. We can ease into our new reality, make accommodations to our age. We can still indulge our love of music, and go to concerts and movies and plays.

So what's wrong with matinees?

The road less traveled

"Will you travel?" There has been a steady drumbeat of questions on this subject since I was widowed a year ago, as if that is what retired people—especially middle-class widowed people—are supposed to do. Join the little old ladies in tennis shoes on a cruise or some kind of an educational tour.

I enjoyed traveling with Bob, but when he became too confused to leave home, I couldn't consider a trip, and even after he was placed in a care facility, I didn't want to leave him. I did get wistful sometimes when friends would describe places they had been or stimulating adventures they had had, but I didn't consider travel an option for me for more than ten years.

Now I am free to go wherever I want (if I can afford it), but frankly the temptation to travel is not nearly as strong as it was when I couldn't go.

Can I navigate the airport with all the new regulations and restrictions? Will I know what to pack? I'm apt to take entirely too much and lug around a big suitcase full of clothes I don't need.

Can I schlepp my own bags?

If I go on a tour, can I keep up with the others? Would I be willing to share a room with a stranger, or have I have lived alone so long that I value my privacy too much?

What fun would it be to visit a secluded location or to be stimulated by new ideas if I couldn't share the experience with someone I love?

I remember when I was always eager to take a trip, to see around the next corner, to try something new. But I can also remember when travel was fun. We dressed up; we were in vacation mode from the time we stepped into the airport taxi. We had actual tickets, and there were helpful people behind clearly marked counters to take them from us. There were skycaps to take our luggage. Planes were roomy enough to tilt our seats back, and there was so much space between rows that we could actually get up to go to the bathroom without landing in somebody's lap. Stewardesses brought pillows and blankets, and the airlines even served real food. No gourmet entrees, to be sure, but better than pretzels and Pepsi. We didn't stand in line for a cattle call. We weren't frisked or bumped from overbooked planes. Once upon a time it was "Bon Voyage" and "Enjoy your trip." Now it's "Move on out."

We get more and more cautious as we age, even as we fight for our independence. Recently I spent two weeks on the North Shore of Lake Superior, a place familiar and much loved. I drove by myself, five hours each way. (What if I have car trouble? What if I get lost?) I stayed in a charming little cabin by the lake where there was no cell phone reception. (How would I get help if I needed it?) I wanted to hike in the woods, as Bob and I used to do, and explore new sections of the Lake Superior Hiking Trail but I held back. (Would anyone know where I was?) I didn't clamber over wet boulders or drive up the Gunflint Trail. I was not as adventurous as once I would have been . . . and I was a bit ashamed.

A couple I know well and admire very much has always loved to travel, and they have had many exciting adventures. But now they go in the company of others. "It only makes sense at our age."

But what is sensible? As we get older it is hard to know when we should push ourselves, stretch and test our limits, or when we need to accept the new strictures that come—inevitably come—with age. When do we fight change, and when do we concentrate on embracing it with as much grace as we can muster?

The questions keep coming and the answers are still elusive. Friends share their travel plans. Schools and colleges offer tempting courses in exotic locations. The mailbox fills with glossy catalogs for river cruises. Ads for winter getaways are sprinkled through newspaper, radio, and TV. The days grow darker and colder. The road beckons.

Is it normal?

Every month or so I get a phone call or someone will approach me at a gathering and ask, "Could we meet for lunch sometime? I want to ask you . . . " My antennae go up. Even before the sentence is finished, I know what the subject of our conversation will be. My caregiver friends have the same experience.

The conversations usually begin, "I am worried about_____." Then a list of symptoms is ticked off and next the painful question, "How do you know?" The truth is, you don't. Is it normal aging? Is it dementia and if so what kind(s)? Alzheimer's, vascular dementia, frontal lobe or posterior cortical atrophy, Lewy body, and MCI are among than fifty kinds of dementia, none of which can be determined except by autopsy. For the person living the questions, the most definitive answer will be "probable Alzheimer's," at least until the symptoms are so pronounced that they can be classified into another category of dementia.

But that does not mean that persons who may be in the beginning stages are helpless! An early diagnosis may be tentative, but it is vital for the well-being of both patient and caregivers. There are many tests to determine mental acuity as we age; there are MRIs to diagram brain function and drugs to manage the symptoms.

If it is (or may be) dementia, there are important issues to be discussed and medical, legal, and financial decisions to be made. In an ideal world, the patient and his or her loved ones sit down for long talks. What kind of medical care does the patient want? What is the best living situation at the present and projected into the future? Who will be responsible for the different aspects of care? Necessary documents are drawn up: wills, health care directives, power of attorney, and a team approach develops. Yes, in an ideal world . . . when the Kingdom comes. The reality is that the partner, spouse, or one adult child is likely to assume all the responsibility, and often that person will feel isolated, scared, or even resentful.

My stepsons loved their dad deeply but they found it so painful to be with him that my biggest fear during our long journey was that I would not outlive him, that there would be no one to supervise his care, and no loving presence to accompany him to the end. (This is not an idle concern, by the way. The staggering statistic from the Alzheimer's Association is that 75 percent of those caring for a demented spouse will die before the patient.)

When friends and family are just beginning to be suspicious, when we want to have lunch and talk, it is very hard for us to look too far down the road. I was given several practical, detailed books about caregiving when Bob was diagnosed, but it was years before I read them. I was doing my best to cope in the present; I didn't want to know what the future would bring. I made all the necessary decisions with professional advice and whatever help Bob could give me. I signed all the documents, and still I tried not to think too far ahead. "Denial is not just a river in Egypt," as they say, but it does let us stay afloat till we are stable enough to tread on rocky ground.

I am always impressed when someone is brave enough to reach out, and I make sure we get together as soon as possible because I remember how long it took me to share my fears with other people. I remember how isolated I felt when his sons brushed aside my concerns, "Dad's fine . . . you know he's always been absent-minded" (true enough). His siblings were incredulous and even his doctor pronounced, "He's too young." I kept silent until our conference minister asked me gently one day as we were driving home from a meeting, "Are you at all worried about Bob?" I remember how grateful I was! I burst into tears. I wasn't crazy after all, something was happening, and I was assured that we would not be alone.

"It takes a village." No one should be alone—not patient, not caregivers. We need to talk with our families and friends, get the best professional advice we can find, and build a community of support.

When shall we meet, dear friend? What's for lunch?

Who cares?

In Britain they are called "carers"—all the staff who work in a
nursing facility, from the administrator to the nurses to the cooks
and maintenance personnel. The term defines who they are, not what
they do. It gives dignity to employees and patients alike, assumes an
equality that our terms "helpers" or "aides" do not.

Like most seniors I want to be cared for and cared about, and for
as long as I am able to be included in decisions about my life. I want
to be respected for the person I have become and the abilities I have
retained. I value my independence. I feel like a child if I have to be helped.
Diminished. You are strong and I am weak, and "I want to do it myself!"

"I don't want to be a burden," you will hear us say. Maybe what we
mean is we don't want to be helped. We don't want you to do chores for
us out of a sense of duty or obligation, resenting the time it takes away
from your busy schedule. We are afraid of dying because it means we
may become unable to speak or move without assistance or even to wipe
our own bottoms—totally dependent on you.

In this country we worship self-reliance. Yet we are inescapably
connected to others, and we are called to be carers all our life. In a
perfect world we would see adults, family and strangers alike, caring
for each other, tending their children and their elders. We would be
called upon to help from a very early age. Care would be something we
could expect to give and be willing to receive for a lifetime. But it is not
quite a perfect world. "If I ever end up like that," says a man visiting his
father in the dementia unit, "just give me a pill. Shoot me!"

What if he could say instead, "I'm here . . . I'll hold your hand . . . I'll
sit with you in the dark of night . . . I'll clean you up. It's hard, yes. But
I will do it for you because I care for you, and someday someone will do
it for me. That's what it means to be human."

When I talk to my daughter-in-law about my fear of being a burden
she says, "Let's find another word! Yes, you may be our responsibility,
you may be a_____" she searches (I suggest pain in the neck). "But you
will not be a burden. You cared for us. We want to care for you."

In a perfect world, everyone would have such a daughter.

Invisible Medicare woman

I know that my experience is not unique. I know that I am whining, but please hear me out. I'm quite sure that I am speaking for many elderly people.

Two years ago I had my left hip replaced and exactly a year later the right one. When I went for the final check-up three months after the second surgery, I told the orthopedic surgeon that my left shoulder had been very sore lately and suggested that since I would be having an X-ray of my hip maybe they could check the shoulder too. When the pictures came back, he shrugged and frowned. "Yep, bone on bone." He said that someday I would need a shoulder replacement. (Huh? Hips and knees I knew about but shoulders?) He admitted that the surgery is not always successful; it is very painful and the recovery is slow. Why would I want to do that? He advised me to wait and gave me a shot of cortisone. "You'll be back," he said.

Three months later I was back for another consultation about the rapidly deteriorating shoulder. "There's nothing else I can do," said the surgeon. "You decide when you are ready." So we talked about pain management. Then I showed him my hands—inflamed, swollen, grotesquely disfigured just in the time since I'd last seen him. OMG. He paid attention.

He referred me to his colleague, the orthopedic hand surgeon. I waited weeks to get in, of course, and when I did that doctor read the hand X-rays and said I would need a thumb replacement on one hand and a fusion on the other. Meanwhile I would qualify for physical therapy and should visit my primary physician.

"How can this happen so fast?" I asked the internist when I finally got in to see him. "Now, Anne, it's not really fast . . . you are old and your joints are wearing out. What did you expect?" He turned back to his computer, typed out the diagnosis, and offered to write prescriptions for pain medicine that I didn't want to fill.

I asked to see a rheumatologist. More X-rays and blood tests, a merry-go-round of doctor visits to the orthopedists and the internist and back. The only medical diagnosis in six months' time is that my shoulder is "terrible" and my hands are "a mess" and I have arthritis—which we've suspected from the beginning. But in the process of seeking a diagnosis I earned my very own health chart on MyCare, as confirmed by an email from DoNotReply.com.

Meanwhile I can no longer raise my arm higher than my waist; I can't hold onto a heavy coffee cup or open jars or buckle my belt or park a car. I have chronic pain that wakes me up at night. The doctors don't confer with one another as they say they will; records don't get sent between offices or posted online the way they are supposed to be; my finger joints are angry, sore, more and more swollen; and no one is taking seriously the threat to my well-being. I feel dismissed, invisible—and angry!

I will not consider any kind of surgery to repair my joints until the doctors know exactly what is ravaging them in the first place. They all agree this is a sensible approach. But they are making no progress with a diagnosis, and I am very scared that the longer it takes, the more permanent the damage will be.

When she was taking my vital signs and doing an interview, a nurse in one of the doctor's offices said to me, "Hmm . . . your blood pressure is good, your cholesterol is normal, you aren't overweight, you look fit . . . I'm not that much younger than you. When was it that you started to fall apart?" I thought for a minute and said it was four years ago. She nodded. "I guess that's about right."

Welcome to the falling apart world of senior health care. Am I paranoid or is this a subliminal message that old people are annoying, that doctors resent Medicare patients who require the most expensive and time-consuming kind of care from their providers? (I too question all the money that is spent on end of life care—but I am not yet ready to place myself at the "end of life!")

When Bob was living with Alzheimer's I was his advocate. Like a mother bear, I protected him from unnecessary painful procedures; I checked to be sure he got his medicines on time, that he was comfortable and warm. When he was in the nursing home I saw to it that he was safe and clean, repositioned to avoid bedsores, well-fed, and his teeth carefully brushed. I had no trouble speaking up for him, but it is much harder to do that for myself. I risk being labeled a cranky and complaining old lady—a bit touched in the head, dearie, don'cha know?

Touched in the head because this old lady seeks long-term relationship with doctor who can be touched in the heart.

HUMMMM!

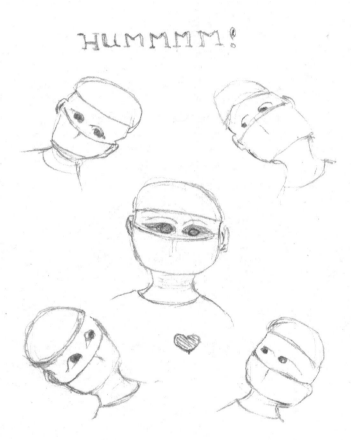

Dancing with Ghosts

All the ghosts of all the lives
I might have lived
waft through my dreams.

Calling from dusty corners of my memory,
We twirl and bow to one another
in the wistful minuet of old age.

4

What's your favorite part of being older?

Five years

It seems a lifetime ago . . . it seems yesterday.

Five years since my beloved partner died. Over time the memories are becoming more comforting than painful. They are everywhere—I hope they always will be.

Bob never lived in this home, and yet I see him all around—in photographs, in the books and music he enjoyed, in presents he gave me, and in letters I saved. I talk to him often.

I can't make this decision alone! What would you do?

How dare you leave when I needed you here?

Thank you for our most amazing life together.

Your kids are doing well.

We miss you!

Like many older people, I am learning to live with ghosts: my parents and grandparents, my sister, my cousin, and the ever-growing list of contemporaries and friends. We keep company with those souls who have left traces in our homes and on our hearts.

Sometimes when I am afraid to try something new or scared to take a risk, my father whispers in my ear using his pet name, "Go, Marv!" If I'm sad, my grandmother caresses my arm with a summer breeze or joins me for a cup of tea. I live alone but I am not lonely when I can open myself to these loving spirits.

With so much of our lives behind us, many of us live in our memories and tell our stories, if we are lucky enough to remember them and to have an audience. We seek out the "thin places" where the spirit world permeates reality. We may be in a different place— emotionally and mentally—and it is tempting to ridicule older people for being out of touch. But we are doing important work, pulling the threads of our life together and stitching past to present and future. Our work needs to be honored and our stories heard before it is too late.

Grandmother packs her suitcase

In her suitcase she puts cosmetics of many different kinds as well as hair dryer, curling iron, and steamer so she can keep up appearances. She has pills and ointments for ailments chronic or imagined, books to entertain her, and iPad and cell phone so she can go one place and stay connected to another.

Grandmother packs a fresh outfit for every day in case something is soiled or torn. So she is prepared for every kind of weather, she also packs a variety of clothing: sandals, hiking boots, sun hat, down vest, the "don't leave home without it" raincoat. She doesn't want to improvise when she arrives at her destination or borrow from her host or have to buy something to fill in. Her suitcase is crammed so tight that there is no room for surprises, and the provisions in it weigh her down.

She rolls the heavy bag into the airport, shuffles it slowly through check-in, waits for it at the baggage carousel after she has landed, then hoists it into a waiting car, straining her arthritic shoulder.

Grandmother lugs a bulging purse over her other shoulder: money, keys, extra pair of glasses, ticket, passport, credit cards, notebook and pens, family pictures. In another compartment there are tissues, sunscreen, hand sanitizer, granola bars, bottled water, toothbrush, airsickness bag, prunes.

When we were children we played the game "Grandmother Packed Her Suitcase," and we imagined everything in there from aardvarks to zebras. Back then I didn't need a suitcase to pack for myself. I put everything I wanted in a backpack and carried it like a turtle; I wore my home and shelter. But now I am the grandmother, and I wonder what happened to the things I carried then: courage, flexibility, faith in the unknown. Whatever happened to throwing caution to the wind and trusting people along the way?

So far I have no reason not to trust. I have been very lucky in my limited travels, and I've even enjoyed some of the perks of being a little old lady. Strapping young men appear out of nowhere to open doors for me, lift my carry-on into the overhead bin, or even to carry my heavy suitcase up or down the escalator. (Where, I wonder, were these handsome guys when I was traveling back and forth to college?)

I am wise enough to know that I might not always get the help I need, especially if I travel alone, and in the middle of the night I can very easily succumb to "what if" thinking. What if I am mugged, my purse stolen, or my cell phone lost? What if I have a stroke or a heart attack and nobody knows where I am—or even who I am?

No matter how we plan, how organized and careful we are, our trip will never go exactly as we expect. We may be annoyed, inconvenienced, scared, delighted, or all of the above by the changes in our itinerary. But that is the point of travel, isn't it? We explore new places inside and out so that we may see in a new way, come home enlightened and refreshed—a different person than the pilgrim who set out on the journey. We learn to depend on our own resources, discovering some we didn't know we had and learn to gratefully accept help from others along the way.

I saw a coffee mug the other day that said, "Life is where what if runs away with why not." I think I need to get that mug so I can be reminded every morning. Grandmothers need to embrace new experiences while we can still enjoy them, accept the risks of growing old, and adapt to changes as they come. And maybe it's okay for us to travel with a suitcase big enough to hold our accumulated wisdom just in case we have an opportunity to share it. Still, I think I had better pack fewer aspirin . . . and more aardvarks.

Too busy to work

A comment often heard from the newly retired: "I'm so busy I don't know how I ever found time to work!" Tossed off in a lighthearted manner, it may indeed be true. Many of us are busy now: caregiving and helping family members do household chores, connecting with old friends, going to classes and exercising to maintain physical and mental health, pursuing hobbies and interests that we have not had the time to indulge until now. We seek meaningful, satisfying activities, and without an outside job to structure our time, we can feel free or overwhelmed and confused.

Some of us trade work for play, taking the time out to which we feel entitled after a lifetime of punching a clock. We move south where the livin' is easy and the golf courses are open year-round.

But whatever we do after we retire, we wrestle with the questions:
Who am I now?
What will I do?
How can I make this last stage of my life meaningful?
We have new freedoms, new choices about how we will spend ourselves, and we can't evade the questions. As we age they circle like buzzards, round and round again.
Who will I be when I can't_____?
What will I do when I lose_____?
How can I create my legacy?

Has-beens

Whoever we were, we are has-beens now. Has-been plumbers and teachers and stay-at-home moms. Has-been artists and athletes and CEOs, otherwise known as PIPs (Previously Important People). Age is the great leveler as our working days come to an end, and we gradually relinquish dreams for our career, redefine ourselves, and measure time from the end. We park past success and failures at the door and focus less and less on what we did, more and more on who we are.

I can look back with 20/20 vision and find a happy, rather surprising integrity to my life. I can see how one major decision influenced another, then another. It all makes sense in retrospect, but who ever could have predicted that this social butterfly from the suburbs would become a sheep farmer? Or that a college dropout from an unchurched family would graduate from seminary?

The best choices I made were those that followed the deepest promptings of my heart or soul. Did I make poor choices and painful mistakes along the way? Indeed. Did I hurt myself and others? Unfortunately yes.

When I held my three "above average" babies, who were (of course) brilliant, artistic, terribly handsome, and wise beyond their days, I wondered what paths their lives would take. If by some chance they decided not to be president of the United States or Mother Teresa or Bill Gates, what would they choose to be? I tried my best to steer them in the "right" way (a.k.a. my way), but if parenting teaches us anything it is that we are not in control—and a good thing that is!

I'm sure that all of us who have the luxury of time to look back and reflect ask ourselves who we would be if we had traveled another road. We wonder if our choices were reckless or wise, deliberate and freely made, or influenced by any number of family and cultural expectations. Were we a spectacular success in this business of living or did we fail miserably—and are we sure we would know the difference?

It doesn't matter now. We are who we have been and "success" is a relative term. It is relational.

All of us want to know that we have made a difference. Even at the very end of his life, in the twilight sleep of Alzheimer's, my dear husband Bob would smile when one of his sons shared a memory or when a friend squeezed his hand and told him that he would be sorely missed.

We have an important challenge, a gift that we can share with one another at the end of our lives. We can be present.

Has-beens unite! We are still Important People.

No regrets

We spend more time now in the museum of our past than in the mysterious cyber future. We create and reform memories, painting our impressions of life as if we could capture them all together into a final masterpiece and display it proudly. Yes . . . this is how it was. This is who I am.

We talk to old friends. "Remember . . . do you remember?"

We go to reunions to see how others have turned out and understand who we ourselves are becoming. How did that mousy little girl in the class behind us become a spiritual leader of the world? Whatever happened to our class president and valedictorian, the boy we voted most likely to succeed?

We mix colors to illustrate connections, working close to the canvas, dabbing here and there, standing back to bring it into focus.

None of us has arrived at old age without being wounded. We have sustained loss of many kinds, made stupid mistakes, wasted our talents, and hurt other people as well as ourselves. "How do you get rid of your regrets?" a friend asked the other day. The answer, I think, is that you don't. You paint them into the picture: bold black lines, grey smudges, white open spaces. We need them all to provide balance and beauty and truth, to highlight the bright splashes of red and yellow, to find forgiveness and grace.

Vocation

He was CEO of a multinational corporation. He had literally thousands of employees, and he loved the business world: visioning, making decisions, managing people, solving problems. He was exceptionally good at it, successful and happy in his work, but he took early retirement to care for his wife who had Alzheimer's. She died recently and he is facing the big question of old age: Who am I now?

I was a caregiver, too, for many years, and I am asking the same question. So are two friends, recent widows, with whom I talk often. All of us have spent the last years, whether at home or at work, doing something that was very important. We have had a purpose. And without that sense of calling, we feel a bit lost.

Can a brilliant and talented CEO find satisfaction in delivering meals-on-wheels?

Will a woman who was actively involved in many community organizations and president of the church council be content to pour coffee and clean up after the worship service?

How can an eighty-four-year-old volunteer be matched to an appropriate need?

The trouble is, we are not willing to settle. We have so little time left that we want to use it well. We feel an urgency to make a contribution to society that somehow, in some manner, seems as important as what we have done in the past. And yet . . . and yet we don't want the long hours, the interruptions, and the demands of jobs we had when we were younger.

We are not looking for a job! Even in old age (or maybe especially now) we want a vocation as Frederick Buechner defines it in his little book *Wishful Thinking: A Theological ABC*: "The place God calls you to is the place where your deep gladness and the world's deep hunger meet."

Good Samaritan

It is the middle of January. I clamber over a snowbank to get to my
car after meeting a friend for lunch. I am carrying a large package
and open the trunk to put it down, tossing my keys on the mat. Then
I scrounge around a bit—among the extra boots, scraper, jumper
cables, kitty litter, and other staples of winter driving in Minnesota—
to make room for the package. Just as I push down on the lid, I
remember my keys. Click! With that sickening sound, I know I have
locked them in the trunk.

Fortunately I am in a very friendly part of town, parked right in
front of the beautiful library in the center square. I go in to call AAA
and wait for the tow truck, which they tell me will take an hour or
more. There are much worse places to be stranded. I can read while
I wait, and I have no plans for the afternoon except to navigate the
unplowed streets back home before it gets dark. I can be patient.

In time a burly young man arrives and tries to pry open the trunk.
He can't get it so he fishes inside the door on the driver's side and
unlocks it but the trunk doesn't open from there without power. He
crawls into the backseat, thinking to push it down and access the
trunk from there. I tell him the back seat doesn't fold down, but he
won't believe me. He pushes switches and pulls cushions, looks up
the car model on his cell phone, and finally calls the dealer. Ruefully
he shakes his head when he hangs up. Now he believes me.

"Do you have another key at home?"

Yes.

"Is there anyone there who could bring it to you? "

No.

He studies me carefully then calls the home office. "I have this
elderly lady here, she lives alone, and I don't know what else to do
except take her back to get a key." For a long time he stands still,
waiting for an answer. It is starting to get dark, and I realize my
heart is pounding. At last Burly nods, hangs up the phone, and smiles
at me, "It's okay. Get in the truck."

As we bump along, we have easy conversations about our favorite radio stations and cars and local politics. He drives me twelve miles home, waits for me to get the key, and then drives me back to my car—the route totally out of his way. When I get back to my car, he refuses to let me tip him. By now it is very dark so this Good Samaritan waits for me to start the engine, then leads me to the ramp where I will enter the freeway.

As I think back on that afternoon I cringe just a bit at the "elderly" description but I will accept it gratefully in return for a free taxi ride. In fact I realize there may be some advantages to my new little-old-lady status. I won't tell many people about this foolish escapade, but I will ponder it for a long time. There are still kind and thoughtful strangers who will help their elders.

Thank you, Burly.

New Year's Day

I feel like a new person, a different woman than I was a year ago. In this last year I have grown OLD. How did that happen? At seventy-five I still thought of myself as middle-aged. I was active, fairly limber, and pain free. I didn't play tennis or ski any more, but I could do pretty much what I had always done and felt pretty much the same as I always had. Three years later, I am more realistic. (Middle-aged? How many 150-year-olds do you know?)

Suddenly my joints are dissolving, attacked by inflammation that the doctors can't get under control. I stoop, I hurt, and I move slowly and shuffle about like the little old lady I would never become. My classmates, too—honor roll students and athletes and class presidents—are dealing with ailments that beset older people but were never supposed to happen to us. We avoid icy sidewalks, don't drive at night, and stay home more and entertain less.

I would have liked to make my signature oyster stew for New Year's and invite friends in for some bubbly, but it is too cold and I am too sore. Perhaps this is why people move to a senior community, so they can have a social life without undue exertion?

I remember New Year's Eve when we were in high school, dancing to records in someone's dimly lit basement, wondering if the boy you liked would kiss you at midnight, afraid he would . . . and afraid he wouldn't. Later there were more glamorous parties and kisses that held promise for the new year, and later still, gatherings of young marrieds with babies and toddlers strewn about the house on every soft surface where they could sleep while their parents watched the ball drop in Times Square. Lastly, a bonfire in front of the church after supper, where we burned bad memories of the old year, wrote resolutions for the new, and ate s'mores.

This year I went to the local deli at 5:00 with my friend Jean. I was home by 7:00 and in bed by 9:00. No kisses at midnight, no bear hugs. And so the years circle back on themselves. In youth, answers and dreams. In old age, memories and questions . . . more questions.

The beat goes on

"Just watch me," the young man said. "Feel the beat!"

Over my protestations that I was too old, I hadn't danced in years,
I didn't know how to dance to the new music . . . he grabbed my hand
and led me to the small dance floor at the end of the banquet hall,
threading our way through the wedding guests and crowded tables.
The DJ was playing some familiar Neil Diamond songs now, and I
had been bouncing in my chair as I took the last nibbles of the bride's
wedding cake. "Sweet Caroline" with full volume and strobe lights! The
room was rocking with energy and festive young dancers.

"Feel the beat" I did. For a few brief moments I forgot that I was the
oldest person in the crowd of three hundred—or maybe second oldest to
the grandmother of the bride. I forgot that I couldn't raise my arthritic
left arm or hold on with my gnarled right hand. I forgot everything
but watching my partner and following his moves. Before I realized it,
my feet moved of their own accord, and I was twirling under his arm,
sliding across the floor, feeling lighter and freer than I have ever felt on
a dance floor.

When I was in junior high, our class went to dancing school. We
were solemnly instructed in the waltz (1-2-3), the foxtrot (step, step,
slide), the box step, and for a raucous good time, the bunny hop. At
home I learned from my mother all the proper etiquette: let the boy
lead, dance with the first one who asks you, always talk to him about
his interests, don't get too close, stay on your toes.

I would go out on a dance floor with my head spinning—thinking,
thinking all the time about whether I was being proper, whether the
boys I wanted to dance with would ask me, if I would step on their
feet—I felt clumsy and slow and restrained and spent an unnecessary
amount of time in the bathroom.

But last night there was no time to think or we would get trampled.
We just moved—quickly, remarkably moved—in time with the music
and the other dancers. It was an out-of-body, out-of-mind experience.
"You are a good dancer," my partner said, and I think I believe him
because for the first time in my life I knew how dancing could feel.

Besides I was proud of myself that I could keep up with him—at least for two dances. I hope no one noticed that I might have been puffing a bit on the way back to the table.

This morning I am flooded with gratitude for the evening I spent with these young people at a wedding I didn't particularly want to attend. (I would hardly know anyone, I wouldn't belong, I'm just an old woman who is the mother of their friend.) Yet I was invited. The bride and the groom and their friends were extremely hospitable, and I was even asked to dance!

Late in life, I have learned a lesson about dancing: there are times to let go, to forget your thoughts and follow your instincts, to get out of yourself and trust the music. I hope that I will be able to dance at my grandchildren's weddings but it is possible that I will never dance again. It doesn't matter. If I have an opportunity in the future I will know what to do. Meanwhile I can look back and understand, even mourn, for my younger self. A lesson learned late is still valuable.

We learn so much from younger people that I am more convinced than ever that we need to live in a community that is made up of all ages. A multigenerational dance where we change who leads and enjoy one another. Elders appreciate being included by younger people. It is very flattering to be asked to do something we are "supposed" to be too old to do. Maybe it makes our children feel good when they give us such pleasure. And it makes us feel good, too, when we can give back, when we have wisdom to share or something we can teach. Hmm . . .

Are there any brides out there who want to learn the Charleston?

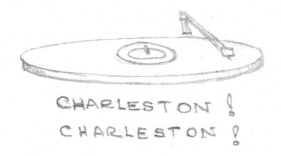

CHARLESTON !
CHARLESTON !

Knit one

I feel my life knitting itself together, almost in spite of me. Stitches dropped over the years are being picked up and formed into a pattern I never envisioned, never even saw.

Sometimes all we need is the glimpse of a pattern taking shape, a day of sunshine when life seems dark or heavy, a sudden moment of lightness and grace.

We see it—and then it is gone. We remember it. Intuitively we search to find those moments again and hold them close forever. But no matter how hard we try, the pattern will change, the threads will unravel . . . and yet we know that they exist. Somewhere loose in the universe, the strands of our lives are being woven into the eternal tapestry.

Sing

Sing to the stars in the cold northern sky
Sing to the waves on the shore
Sing to the grasses that curtsey and sigh
To the winds that whisper and roar.

Sing to the mountains, the forest, the plain
To tall buildings and wide open sky
Through hurricane, famine, and drought sing your pain
In harvest abundance sing joy.

For the life we've been given, the life that we choose
The surprises that each day may bring
For the talents we waste and the talents we use
Bow down, stand tall and sing.

5

What are your thoughts on modern technology?

Changing times

I am eighty years old. I have had two hips replaced, and I am standing on the top step of a six-foot ladder in front of the back door trying to change the battery of the alarm system in my condo. Carefully I pry open the case.

Bells ring! Lights flash!

I clamber down and run (as swiftly as a bionic woman of my age can run) to the keypad by the front door. WARNING: Broken glass! FAULT . . . FAULT . . . FAULT . . .

Well I know the glass is not broken, and I manage to turn off the alarm before I get an emergency call. But I also know that I will have to hire someone from the alarm company to come and install my new battery.

It will take three to four days to get through the phone system. One recording will inform me that all representatives are helping other customers, and another one will explain that all repairmen are busy with other service calls. But that same friendly voice will assure me that my call is very important and I can leave a message. Eventually I will get an appointment for a service call with a four-hour window. The weather will be glorious, of course, and I will wait inside for three hours and fifty-nine minutes, and then I'll be charged an exorbitant price, but at least the system will work. By the time the new battery runs low, I'm sure I will have forgotten again how to change it so the process will repeat itself. I always forget how to reset the clock in my car to spring forward or fall back when the seasons change, and as a last resort I have to get out the manual.

I miss the days when there was a man in my household: father, husband, son. When the "little woman" was not expected to climb ladders and change batteries or repair machinery or clean gutters. At the same time, I'm sure there are many older men who took pride in their ability to do household chores and feel displaced now because they are physically unable to help.

In order to get the services we need, we will have to hire someone to do them or move to a continuing care community. "Please listen carefully as the options have recently changed . . . "

Retrieving messages

I am on the first day of a two-week vacation by myself—visiting Grand Marais, the community where Bob and I used to live. I will have time to spend with old friends, to walk on the beaches and in the woods, and to read and write. I am staying in a cozy cabin on the shore of Lake Superior. It is a beautiful setting and I am excited to be here! I have unpacked and settled in.

But not "settled in" the way I did as a child when we went on family vacations. Wherever we were on those trips the first thing my sisters and I did was to go exploring. We dutifully hauled our duffle bags or suitcases, toys, and games into the room we would share, and then with a great slamming of doors and tunings out of warnings "be careful" and "don't go too far," we would escape outside.

If we were staying someplace where we had been before, we hunted for our favorite little nooks, secret hiding places, and we compared this year to others past: Has that tree grown taller? Are there any agates on the beach? Remember when . . . ? If we were in a new place, we shared our discoveries with each other and then with our parents, chattering about them all through supper. We were enchanted by everything that was new and different and mysterious.

But now, here in this cabin whose familiarity comforts me, I am not ready to explore. I am retrieving messages on my iPad and charging my cell phone, making sure that I am closely connected to the very world I am trying to vacate. I am afraid of forgetting things, of being forgotten, of getting lost. I wonder if these feelings can be attributed to a certain lack of confidence and fear of the unknown that is beginning to nibble away at my independence as I grow older. Or if I am more dependent on modern technology than I would like to admit.

The other day I was waiting in my doctor's office when a mother walked in with her two teenage daughters. You could tell they were related by their physical resemblance but nothing in their manner would have indicated that they knew each other. There they sat, for twenty minutes, side by side on the upholstered leather bench, all three punching buttons on their phones: texting, emailing, retrieving messages without speaking a word.

I have seen young couples at a restaurant, phones in hand, sharing information that streams to them through cyberspace. Whatever happened to conversation that is real, immediate, and personal? Do families have noisy dinner tables any more? For that matter, do they eat dinner together?

I am discovering that the Wi-Fi reception in my cabin is unpredictable, that cell phones don't work except when there is a clear view of the lake, and that email is sent on an offshore breeze. I am going to be forced to unplug.

Hello, birch trees. Hello, waves splashing on giant boulders.

Here I come.

I have a lot to explore.

Number, please?

Sometimes I wonder what my grandmother would think of today's telephones. She had the two-handed kind, where she held the earpiece in her right hand and the receiver in her left. When she first lifted the earpiece off the receiver, an operator came on the line to ask, "Number please?" Hers was eighty-four; ours was twenty-eight.

The phone was tucked into a little closet under her stairs, a painful walk from the living room or bedroom when she was crippled with arthritis. She lived ten miles from her children but in a different zone and every call to them cost her ten cents. On the other hand, they could call her for free (who knows why?), and when they did she would exclaim, "Oh, dearie! I've been waiting soooo long to talk to you!" She would pull up her little chair and settle in for a chat, hunched over to speak directly into the mouthpiece.

There was a common etiquette for phone calls in those days. You never called before 9:00 a.m. or after 9:00 p.m. It was extravagant to call long distance, but my parents allowed it once in a while—station to station only, short calls, on Sunday when the rates were lower. Person to person calls, daytime calls—everyone knew those were an emergency.

When I was a teenager, we got a dial telephone for our house, with a heavy base and a long cord that I could thread from a pass-through in the kitchen into the coat closet. I would lie on a pillow in a nest of boots and shoes and talk for hours to the friends I had just seen all day at school. There were lots of secrets in those giggly, rambling talks—or so we thought. But conversations were not very private then, especially in the country where neighbors could eavesdrop on your party line.

Gradually phones became touchtone, numbers were enlarged to seven digits and then ten. As mothers of young children, my friends and I installed wall phones in the kitchen with cords as long as jump ropes so we could chase after noisy toddlers or investigate why the house suddenly went quiet as we were talking. There was precious little privacy in those days, too, but there is even less now.

Today everything I ever wanted to know about almost anybody (and in some cases a great deal more) is available on my phone. I have instant access to Facebook, email, text messages, and Google in my pocket. My phone is a clock, a calendar, an encyclopedia, a checkbook, and a map. I can be interrupted by my ringtone or distracted by others' wherever I go—to the grocery store, a restaurant, a meeting, on the street, or in my car. We are so used to the distraction that we have to be reminded to turn off our phones in concerts or movies, even in church. Our cell numbers aren't listed in a directory, but somehow nonprofits and community organizations get ahold of them, and we are bombarded by solicitations and recorded messages.

I am (mostly) grateful for electronics, and I depend heavily on my phone, but sometimes I would just like to yell, "Stop! Stop the virtual world, I want to get off!"

I want to settle all by myself into a closet under the stairs and dial my way home.

Long enough

When she was nearing the end of her days, my grandmother said, "I think, my dear, that I have lived long enough." In her rich life she had seen Americans travel the Oregon Trail and land on the moon. She had driven a horse and buggy, and she had ridden in a minivan. She had followed the fashions of Gibson girls, the New Look, and miniskirts. "I don't understand the world any more," she told me. As often happens, I didn't appreciate what she was saying at the time. But elders grow wiser as I age.

Unlike my children and grandchildren, I do not get excited about new technology. I write with a #2 pencil on a yellow legal pad. I don't sit in front of a screen when I can be at the kitchen table with my coffee cup at hand or sprawl in a lounge chair on my deck. I don't know how to tweet on Twitter or blog and I don't want to learn. I treasure my friends too much to befriend any of them on Facebook.

I learn only what I have to learn to keep one foot in the twenty-first century. I can correspond by email and do basic word processing. I take the free lessons that come with my new Apple computer and leave every session wondering what I accomplished. A nice young kid, just out of diapers, has shown me shortcuts and bells and whistles that I can't remember by the time I get home. (Fortunately when I go back next week, I will meet with some other kid who won't know that I have asked the very same questions before). When finally I master a new skill, the program changes or the software is updated, and I have to start all over again.

When my aunt was younger than I am now, she was driving a car that was many years old. It had a few dings on the outside and some hiccups under the hood, but it suited her just fine, thank you. She understood her vehicle. My uncle, who always drove a late model car, wanted to replace Old Faithful but she would have none of it: "I'll drive it till it dies!" I thought she was crazy of course. Who wouldn't want a spanking new car, your own choice of model and color?

Well, for one, I wouldn't . . . not any more. I have a wonderful five-year old coupe that is very comfortable and easy to handle. The fender may be a tiny bit dented (I park by feel) and it has fairly high mileage, but overall it is in good shape and reliable. It is polite and responsive and doesn't send false alarms or talk back to me through Blue Teeth.

The door opens with a key, the radio turns on with a knob, and without an engineering degree, I can even set the clock back when we go off daylight saving time. It gets almost thirty mpg, and I like the dealer where I get service. So why would I want to replace it? Until automobiles can be manufactured to run on air or find themselves in a crowded parking ramp, I'll stick with what I have.

I haven't yet lived quite "long enough," but like my aunt and my grandmother I think change in old age is highly overrated.

Evolution

The father who is enormously successful in business, who urges his sons to enter the corporate world, becomes the grandfather who encourages grandsons to follow their hearts. Making a life is more important than making a living, he tells them.

The mother who does not allow her daughters to leave the house in blue jeans, except for sports or camping, becomes the grandmother who invites her blue-haired, jean-clad granddaughter to a fancy restaurant for dinner; the same woman who scolded her daughter for holding hands in public with her fiancé helps a granddaughter move in with her boyfriend.

Our children must wonder, wistfully sometimes, how these patient, good-humored grandparents evolved from the strict and stolid parents they knew growing up. Where were we when they most needed our acceptance and understanding?

Little do they know that we are wondering too. Wondering how those noisy and demanding toddlers, those self-absorbed adolescents, have become such patient and loving parents. How did they turn into attentive caregivers for the mother or father they would hardly acknowledge, it seems, just a few years ago?

It's evolution . . . it's a puzzle . . . it's a miracle.

Where did all the people go?

Where are the parking ramps where I could drive up to a booth at the entrance and some energetic young man would magically appear to give me a claim check and park the car, then retrieve it for me politely, for a small tip, when I was ready to leave?

Now I get an automated ticket from a machine I can't reach without half climbing out the car window. When I leave I pay at another machine with my credit card, then put the ticket—right side up, stripe on the left, into a third machine that will tell me to have a good day if I finally do it right and don't drop it on the grungy floor I am trying to reach across.

Where are the real live people who answered the telephone without making me wait while a recording told me how important my call was? The other day I wanted to buy an airplane ticket. It was a complicated procedure. I had to cancel my original plans because of a broken wrist, redeem that ticket and then buy one for a later date, and collect travel insurance for the cancelled flight. I tried to do it online but it was too confusing, so I made a call to the airline . . . waited . . . and waited while the call was monitored for quality purposes and then (final indignity!) I was billed twenty-five dollars on my credit card for talking to a person instead of a computer.

Where are the salesclerks who ask if they can help us instead of turning their backs to the customers and gossiping at the back of the store? Where are the checkout boys who offer to carry grocery bags to our cars without mumbling reluctantly?

Where are the doctors' offices that identify us by name instead of insurance policy? Where is the staff that will treat an elder like a whole human being instead of a twelve-minute Medicare checkup? Does anyone but the very old remember when doctors made house calls? Looked at patients instead of their computer screens?

Where is the bank teller who doesn't call a supervisor and require two forms of identification before permitting us to withdraw money from our own accounts? An ATM is faster and more personal. One September when I was out of state and inserted my debit card, the machine flashed *Happy Birthday!* across the screen.

Whatever happened, twenty-first century technology can't be undone. If I were running the world, I would replace robots with real people who can't find employment. But I am not running the world, which is a good thing too. Our economy would be in even more of a shambles than it is. The next generations cut their teeth on technology, and they will know how to put it to good use. My hope is that they will challenge our priorities and show all of us how to put people first.

Really??

I didn't mean to eavesdrop but their voices were loud as they talked to each other and wandered about the coffee shop, laughing and taking calls on their cell phones. I felt they were rude, but their confidences were safe with me . . . I had no idea what they were, like, you know, talking about.

This is the season of Downton Abbey and I am addicted. The perfect English, the lovely clipped accents of the nobility, their manners and civility, even their cunning ways of manipulating people and events make me nostalgic for a time I never knew. I feel more at home in that make-believe world than I do with the slang and grunts and four-letter words that make up conversation on our screens and in our streets.

Maybe that is what happens as we age. Increasingly we feel that the world we knew is disappearing, and we don't understand the one that is taking its place.

Third graders no longer learn handwriting by the Palmer Method; they touch screens. They don't write or talk in whole sentences; BTW, they text. I am a stranger in my homeland.

The other day I drove by the home where I grew up. The road has been rerouted, the trees have grown so tall they obscure the driveway, and I went right by without recognizing it. And what is true geographically is true socially. The milestones are gone. I navigate without a compass.

Last night I was watching the Olympics. An announcer commented about a skier in the women's moguls competition, "She went huge on the top air!" HUH?

Earlier in the day I had filled out a form for my medical history. Check one:

Man_____ Woman_____ Other_____
REALLY?

What's in a name?

When we were quite young children, my sisters and I were taught very strict protocol about how to relate to adults. If they came into the room where we were playing, we must scramble to our feet and greet them. When we were introduced to visitors, friends of our parents or grandparents, we must look the person straight in the eye, offer a firm handshake, or even (roll your eyes!) drop a curtsey. We must address the persons by name: Mr. _____ or Mrs. _____, never by the first name unless we knew them well and were invited to add an honorary Aunt or Uncle.

Today I am almost always addressed by my first name—and by whippersnappers forty to fifty years younger than I! "Hello, Anne," says my new dentist, introducing himself. "I am Dr. Drill." He looks like a high school student but the diplomas on his wall prove that Dr. Drill deserves the title. He deserves his, but as his elder and a new patient, as a perfect stranger, I think I also deserve mine.

Years ago my friend Sheila's grandmother, a bright and proper and very elegant lady in her nineties, was admitted to a nursing facility with advanced Parkinson's. Soon after she arrived, an eager young nurse walked into her room. "Good morning, Hazel," she beamed. "I've brought you a yummy breakfast." The old woman lifted her plate of scrambled eggs and, despite her severe tremor, threw it across the room like a Frisbee. "I am not Hazel to you. I am Mrs. Brooks!"

I swallow hard when I am greeted by a three-year-old with "Hi, Anne!" as I walk into church. But I try to smile broadly because I'm extremely grateful for the spontaneity and the welcome.

I take great pride in introducing my children and grandchildren to my friends. I want to do it in a way that is both contemporary and respectful. But the rules are not as clear as they used to be. For instance, if Susie Jones marries Bob Smith but keeps her maiden name, do I introduce her as Mrs. or Ms. If she uses both names is she Jones-Smith or Smith-Jones . . . or does she have a new combination? What she is not at this first meeting, at least as far as I am concerned, is "Susie." I would feel presumptuous introducing her that way.

When Queen Elizabeth of England celebrated her sixtieth jubilee, I saw on TV a stream of commoners and heads of state alike, greeting her with a curtsey or a bow (not a single "howzit goin', Liz?"), and I watched her gracious response. I know it marks me as a dodo, and I am hopelessly out of touch, but I would like to see some of those manners in this country. It is not the majesty or the pomp, it is very simply the respect—for the person, for her position, and in this age of instant intimacy and Facebook friends, for the appropriate formality of our relationship.

Multitasking

Raising young children—it was part of the job, but I've known for a long time that I can't multitask any more. I don't even read a book and listen to music at the same time. Now I like to pay bills, file receipts, and put away the checkbook before I start the next project. Answer emails, make phone calls, do errands—one at a time. If I am interrupted I feel anxious, afraid I will forget something. I have envied young people who can juggle many jobs at once. They walk fast, talk fast, and get an amazing amount accomplished in a very short time.

But there is a limit, even for them.

The other day I was in a public bathroom. A young mother had just gone into the stall next to mine with her toddler in a stroller, two big satchels, and a heavy coat. She was sitting on the toilet, talking on her cell phone. Talking loudly so she could be heard over the flushing toilets. "Just a minute," I heard her say. Then . . .

"EEEK!" A splash. Silence . . . "Are you still there? I dropped the phone in the toilet!"

Busted!

For Christmas this year my grandson, a college freshman, gave me a morning of tech support. What a gift! Evan came to my home, set me up with Skype, ordered an airline ticket, synched and surfed, and taught me shortcuts. He cheerfully and patiently answered questions that must have seemed unbelievably simple to him. In the process he discovered my passwords. Oops!

As he burst into gales of laughter, I explained that the words were variations on my college nickname—a name I cherished fifty years ago but left behind for reasons that would be very obvious if I told you what it was.

After our session he took me out for lunch—snickering, teasing, addressing me by my "new" old name and making me laugh right out loud.

I think I'm stuck with it now . . . funny I don't mind at all. For one thing, I will never be confused with another grandma as the children marry and their families grow. And for another, the people who know me by my nickname are special friends from a very specific time in my life. All past associations are good and now they are embellished by memories of that wonderful winter morning.

Grandchildren are the gift and reward of old age. Stories passed down through the ages bind us together as life moves forward, yet circles back on itself.

What's in a name? Love and laughter and belonging and . . . maybe a little blackmail.

Late Life Love

It is a gentling,
a letting down easy,
a banking of warm embers
after the blaze of youth.

It is opening the door
when you come home,
knowing that someone inside
will be happy to see you.

It is meatloaf and mashed potatoes,
one small glass of wine
and talking about your day.
It is sitting on the couch

at opposite ends,
each with your own reading light,
knowing that she will doze off
before you go to bed

and knowing, too,
how the curve of her back
will fill the spoon of your body
while you sleep.

It is sowing dreams
and harvesting memories
and protecting every fragile tendril
of the present.

It is the comfort of familiar haunts
and family patterns
and understandings between old friends
that are deeper than words.

It is freedom shackled to failing health,
giving and receiving care . . .
determined independence
reaching for an outstretched hand.

In a home with two heartbeats
it is mature souls
losing and laughing,
holding on and learning to let go.

6

Do you see parallels between what was cool when you were young and what's cool today?

It's important

I have lunch with a couple in their fifties whom I have known and loved for years. We talk about my manuscript, and I ask what they would like to know about aging.

"Sex," says the husband.

WHAT?

"Well," he says with a wink at his wife across the table. "I want to know what older people do about sex. It's important!"

Now this is a subject I had not thought to address. It's not one that I talk to friends about directly, though we dance around the edges. I can share some impressions and observations, then let the reader fill in the blanks.

One thing I know from a long and happy marriage is that sex takes on new meanings when we age together. We don't engage in it for procreation, after all, and whether gay or straight, we are no longer driven by raging hormones. Sex becomes an expression of love and commitment and trust. It is the comfort of familiarity, "one flesh"— and no less exciting for that.

But what happens when we are left alone?

What I miss the very most is touch. When I have been gone all day, Bob is not there to welcome me home with a kiss . . . to hold me if I am tired or sad or confused. There is no one to rejoice with on occasions that call for high fives and hugs . . . no arm around my waist when we walk into a crowd . . . no hand to squeeze . . . no warm body cuddling next to me in bed. When I reach out in my sleep, there is only a pillow. One flesh torn in two.

We all know that many older people live alone, "almost half of all elderly people" (over sixty) according to a poll by *The Telegraph* (12/22/2011). Some are alone by choice; others by necessity. But all of us must make accommodations to different stages in our lives.

Some of us learn to enjoy solitude; others join match.com, hoping to marry again. I know several couples who lead independent lives during the week and then spend weekends together. Often they are travel companions as well. Since we are not bound by social norms or the obligations of raising a family, many configurations are possible, and sex can take different forms. Elders may be as liberated now as women were in the sixties when the pill came out. We can shack up, hook up, become significant others, or FWBs.

If we are partnered, now is the time to talk openly about our changing needs and what gives us pleasure. We may make adaptations because of health issues, and if we do, according to a nurse practitioner I know well, it is possible to enjoy sex well into our nineties. Rejoice!

But my thoroughly unscientific, intuitive conviction is that what we crave when we grow old is not sex—if by sex we mean intercourse—it is intimacy. In time our physical needs and abilities will wane, no matter what our situation. But our emotional needs will wax full. We need to feel safe. We need to feel connected to friends and family and to a world beyond ourselves.

We may not ever know that certain special touch again, and for all our lives we will miss it, but now that we are older we can reach out to many others and touch them without sexual implications. Same sex, mixed gender —we are as free to hug as to shake hands.

But as our flesh shrivels and dries, will anyone want to touch us? I worry about that sometimes, and I suspect others do too. There is an elderly widow in our congregation who says that passing the peace is her favorite part of Sunday worship. "It's the only time all week that anyone touches me."

I have seen families and even caregivers in nursing homes who are reluctant to get physically close to their patients. Yet our first sense of the world is touch, and it may be the last sense that remains. We can and we must hold each other—hold on tight.

It's important!

Birthday club

I wonder what the young women are thinking. They are gathering at a large table in the middle of the room, within direct view of the "old Fuddies" seated in the back corner. They have breezed into our favorite restaurant on a lunch break from work. They are sharply dressed, effusive, fast-talking, and energetic, grabbing a quick bite before they head back to offices somewhere in the vicinity.

We are deliberate and slow, quietly mulling over the menu and comparing choices. Probably they hope they will never look like us, never be so slow or old, never have conversations that are quite so boring: the weather, children and grandchildren, aches and pains.

They might be surprised to learn that we talk about the same things they do.

We haven't been together for awhile, so first we catch up on each others' lives and that includes our health—mental, emotional, physical. Of course we talk about our families! The young women do too. But while they are passing cell phones around the table to show pictures of their children, we are discussing not the decline and fall of families as they "used to be," but subjects that weren't even on our radar screens when we were their age: gay marriage, sperm banks and IVF, surrogate parenting. We are remarkably open to new practices and grateful that two of us have grandchildren who were conceived through the miracles of modern medicine.

We, too, talk about trying to balance family time with work—both in the younger generation and in our own. Some of us are still employed; the others do a wide variety of volunteer work.

As women at the other table chatter about their business trips, one of us describes her recent vacation to a third world country, and then accompanied by raucous laughter we debate the best tactics for peeing in the outback: wear a long skirt, always carry a tissue in your pocket, pack a funnel.

At both tables, we share news of our friends, only at ours we help each other fill in the blanks. "I saw _____ with a handsome white-haired man the other day. How is _____ doing? Whatever happened to _____?"

Like younger women, we talk about fashion. Forget the three-inch spike heels—we want to know where to get sturdy, comfortable shoes at a reasonable price or jeans that come up to the navel and skirts that go down to the knee.

"What have you been reading lately? Are you taking any classes? What do you think of our political situation?" (We shake our heads over that subject.) The questions are ageless.

The younger women pay separate bills for their salads, stand, wave, and bustle out the door. The waitress clears our plates while we have a second cup of coffee and debate whether to have dessert. After a long discussion about the evils of cholesterol and fats and sugars, we defer to the "birthday girl" who on cue orders a large portion of the richest dessert on the menu with five forks. We savor every guilty mouthful and then without a quibble, treat her by splitting the bill for five into four.

The restaurant is quiet now. Time to go. It has been a lovely get-together and a delicious meal. I have thoroughly enjoyed the outing but once a day is enough for me. I need the social stimulation, and I also appreciate my private time. Now I will go home, change my clothes, and read a book and relax, basking in the warmth of these friendships all afternoon. Those young women will go back to work for several hours and then face the demands of housework and family care long into the evening after they get home.

I've "been there." So have all the other women in the birthday club. I'm sure that none of us could or would keep such a schedule again. If that makes us old and boring, so be it. But if I were a young woman, it's possible that I might envy us.

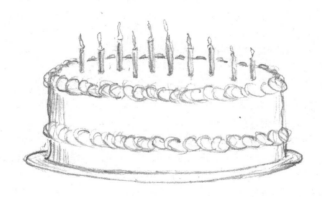

Fifty years ago

The memory is vivid still.

It is 6:00 on an evening during the week. I am standing in the kitchen, one baby on my hip and another toddling beneath my feet. I am stirring a pot of spaghetti; around the corner diapers are whirling in the dryer; the dog is whining to go out; the phone is ringing; and my husband's car pulls into the garage. He walks through the kitchen, pecks my cheek, and keeps going into his den. He closes the door. It's been a hard day at work. Poor dear. He needs time out. I try to quiet the hungry children, answer the phone, and keep stirring the pot . . . inside I am screaming, "For THIS I studied four years of Latin?"

I share the memory at a gathering of college classmates. Eyes light up. Heads nod. Yes! All of us had felt that way.

We were privileged women. We were given the opportunity to go to college in an era when higher education for girls was not taken for granted. We were expected to study hard, to be firmly grounded in the liberal arts, and, incidentally, to meet boys from "good families," one of whom we would marry soon after graduation.

As a young girl, I had dreams. If I was asked what I wanted to be when I grew up, I might have said world traveler, an interpreter for the United Nations, a journalist, or a veterinarian. But as I grew older, the dreams evaporated and I walked with willing steps into the future that was expected of me. Some of my classmates cannot remember wondering at all about what they would be when they grew up. We were supposed to know. It was in the air we breathed.

We would marry successful men, stay at home to raise above-average children, and be dedicated volunteers in our community. Shows like *Leave It to Beaver* and *Father Knows Best* showed us how to be cunning housewives, keeping the family fed, clothed, and calm so our husbands were free to do important work at the office.

The irony is that I never studied the role I was destined to play. My mother went to college, and she was determined that I too would have a good education. (Was she ever asked what she wanted to be when she grew up?) Learning the domestic arts would come later— on the job training, no instruction manual, independent study.

If I could read, I could cook. I would learn how to care for babies by having one. I could practice housekeeping by picking up my room, please. And I could turn my attention to history and art and organic chemistry. I loved school and was grateful for my education then; I am profoundly grateful now. But for many years I felt disintegrated.

The 1960s changed all that. In our thirties and forties we allowed ourselves to question everything. Options exploded all around us as we tried on different roles. Freedom was blowin' in the wind. Families and societies were splintered.

Looking back, I realize how much pressure there must have been on men who were expected to "bring home the bacon," to be a good provider for the family, and take care of the little woman. All of us were trapped by our limited choices and yet sometimes I wonder if we were more free than young people today who feel they can and must have and do it all.

My granddaughter studies Latin and she makes a mean chocolate banana cake. She is a soccer star who can practice her moves behind a vacuum cleaner. She plans a career in medicine. I admire her enormously. I envy her. And sometimes I just want to put my arms around her and say:

Be who you are.

Love what you do.

Life is a giant puzzle. But the pieces fit . . . somehow all the pieces fit.

Making sense

I have lost my sense of smell. When I walk around the neighborhood and pass a bed of roses or a newly mown lawn, I can't enjoy the fragrance. I overseason food because I don't taste it the way I used to, and I have to be careful to follow recipes exactly when I cook for someone else. Losing this sense has narrowed my world somewhat but I count myself lucky. I have friends with macular degeneration and hearing loss and neuropathy.

What do we do when we begin to lose touch with our environment? We make accommodations—that's what!

In his book *What Are Old People For: How Elders Will Save the World*, Dr. William Thomas writes:

> Keeping a human body upright and moving is a spectacular feat of coordination and reaction under any circumstances. Watch and marvel. Miracles are all around you, once you know where to look. The adaptive strategies employed by older adults are routinely misinterpreted as inferior copies of youth's gold standard. . . . These new skills and capacities are subtle and they are routinely overlooked or dismissed outright, even by older people themselves. They are also important, even vital, to our well-being (Vanderwyk and Burnham, 2007, p. 25).

I think of the woman in my neighborhood who lists as she walks, paddling the air with one hand to propel herself forward. Clumsy and awkward, yes. But she walks! She knows that it is vital to her well-being, so every day, all year round, she braves the elements. It is no small accomplishment to walk in a blustery Minnesota winter on icy sidewalks with snowdrifts piled high on either side.

I know many people who are trying to adjust to hearing aids. They are uncomfortable, hard to insert, and hard to get used to. The volume and direction of sound is difficult to control, and they are expensive. But these seniors are determined to adapt because the alternative is to live in a silent world.

We may order books on tape when we have trouble reading, slow our gait and accept the necessity of using a walker or wheelchair, swallow our pride and gratefully hold on to a companion's arm when we are out and about or order a necker's knob (google it!) so we can drive. We do not want pity or denigration for our elderly state. We want respect and credit for our creative adaptability. Growing old is a steep learning curve!

First person singular

"I'm only half a person," says a friend who is recently widowed.

"Half a couple," I try to correct him gently. "You are still a whole person."

"Well, I don't feel like it!"

I know exactly what he means.

The echo of a home without two heartbeats

The anxiety of walking alone into a crowded room

Eating dinner with the news hour for companionship

Staying home from concerts or movies or other special events because it is not fun to go alone

Untethered freedom to make plans—to eat, sleep, work, stay in, or go out

Being the only member of the oldest generation at family gatherings

The lack of identity when we are not defined by our commitments to another

"I" is a lonely word! Both my friend and I miss the presence of a beloved partner—the voice, the footsteps, the touch—the constraints and the comfort of "WE."

Y's woman

The old woman shuffles into the YWCA, bent over, leaning heavily on her cane. She stops at the desk to check in, taking her turn in line with all the lithe twenty-somethings in their tight spandex with firm abs. Being "Minnesota Nice," most of them defer to her, holding the doors, waiting patiently while she digs through purse and pockets to find her membership card. But you know they are rolling their eyes and whispering to each other, "Why does she bother to come here? Someone like that, she'll never get in shape."

At the back of the room, some seniors with a different perspective are standing by the treadmills. "What a brave woman! I guess I can't complain about my problems."

All of us want to stand tall, walk briskly, and exercise rigorously, to be independent and pain free till the end of our days. Of course. But those of a certain age recognize that the odds are against us. By the time we are eligible for Medicare we have a preexisting condition. In fact, we ARE a preexisting condition! It is called OLD. No longer can we expect to be cured of every ache and pain or put back together like Humpty Dumpty. We will learn (probably the hard way) to balance what we can expect to have and do with what we want. Even if we exercise and eat well, we will need to have tune-ups or parts replaced or nicks and dents repaired. We can't turn back the odometer.

Surely the woman at the Y had help with transportation this morning, and she may have needed assistance in bathing, dressing, or cooking as well. I'm sure all of us thought to ourselves, "I hope I don't end up like that!" But do we really?

I hope that when I am caught up like that woman by my preexisting condition, I will be able to accept help. I hope I will have her courage and humility and resourcefulness. She does what she can do; she gets out and about in public. She goes in her own way and at her own speed. Clumsy and slow, she gives new meaning to the term aging gracefully.

Downsizing

Surrounded by cardboard boxes
of every shape and size,
he kneels on the bare wood floor
burrowing into his past—
sixty years of artwork, letters, cards, and photographs.

He does homage to his life
piecing it together . . .
to preserve
display
pass down.

She tucks painful memories
into creases and pockets of the clothes
she will take to Goodwill,
as if a stranger could inhabit
her cast-off dreams.

She will mend and polish others,
make alterations to the truth
try it on
adjust
and preen.

While he venerates the past
she reinvents it,
trying as we all do,
to determine
how they will be remembered.

Does age really bring wisdom?

The more things change . . .

. . . the more they remain the same. A pithy little comment, a glib response—easy to say and hard to hear—especially if we don't want to know that it is true.

I don't like change! I don't want my comfortable routine disrupted. I like things to remain "just the way they are." I remember my first experience of freedom and the challenge of college, later a household of boisterous children, then quiet days with my beloved when he was still strong and healthy and bright. Different as they were, I look back on each of these wonderful periods wistfully, forgetting that there were difficult transitions in between.

Now I am in transition again, from a middle-aged woman to a senior citizen. Where once I had leadership roles in church and community organizations, I have become invisible. Once the multitasking mom and domestic engineer of our family, I am now the matriarch in orbit around my children and grandchildren. It is a joyous role and one that makes me very proud, but even good change produces anxiety, loss of control, and fear of the unknown.

How did I get here? Where am I going? Who am I, now that I am old?

With every technological invention, the world seems to tilt. With new medical discoveries, family milestones, and changes in our environment we are thrown off balance. Where is our fulcrum?

We reinvent ourselves; we count on loved ones—family and friends. But they, too, grow old or die or move away. (Stop! Please! Don't leave me.) We count on physical health and mental acuity to solve our problems, but we suspect that eventually we will be betrayed by both mind and body. We burden ourselves with an accumulation of the years—possessions of material value, sentimental "stuff" to remind us of the good old days—and then pack them away in a storage locker.

Yet all the while that we are looking outside for answers to "life's persistent questions" (as Garrison Keillor would say), there is something inside us that does not change.

If we can dig through all the years of false expectations, of pleasing others and following rules, trying to behave and to belong, we will find that little nugget of ourselves. If we can slow down and trust the silence, we will hear what Elijah calls "the still small voice," and we will recognize it because it is our voice and for all our lives it has been whispering, gently trying to get our attention.

Things will never again be "the way they were"—comfortable and familiar and safe. I will have to find another path through the world. It may not be the path I would choose, and I may have a hard time adjusting to this change. But I have fallen before and I have landed— sometimes with a soft and graceful landing, sometimes with a painful thud. Still, I have survived the fall. So far, some things remain the same.

Finding home

I am taking a sabbath day, a holy time out. On a dark and unseasonably cold April morning, I drive out into the country to visit with a friend. We sit in front of her log fire, share a leisurely lunch of homemade soup and bread, and we talk . . . talk for hours, catching up on each other's lives. Then it begins to snow so I decide to try a different, shorter way home.

There are lots of twists and turns, but I am almost sure I can find my way. After all in addition to my friend's very explicit directions, I have a GPS in the car and, in my purse, a phone that is smarter than I am—complete with Google maps. But I go ten miles, miss a turn somewhere, and . . . I am totally lost. Nothing looks familiar. I don't even know what road I am on or which direction I am headed. There is a cold lump in the pit of my stomach. I am ready to cry.

I have always had a poor sense of direction. My cousin is equally bad so we assure ourselves that it runs in the family, and we have always been this way. Bob used to advise me to "follow your instincts and do the opposite." So this helpless, stupid, panicked feeling is nothing new. If it were, my children would be justified in taking my car keys. But knowing that I am navigationally challenged is little solace now. I have to pull myself together. I want to go home!

Suddenly I find myself thinking about our lunch conversation. My friend, impatient with and concerned about her parents confides, "Dad is getting so forgetful! I don't think he should manage the checkbook anymore but I don't know how to take it away from him . . . and Mom? She's trying to use a computer and she can hardly handle Publishers Clearing House!"

In an instant I understand how those parents must feel. They are as frightened and lost as I am, their habitual jobs and tasks are no longer familiar, and they are losing their skills to cope. But their condition will not improve, and they will try to hide it. If they appear weak and vulnerable, the well-meaning children will step in and take away their independence. "Buzzards," their father calls them when they try to help.

But they need help as I do to find my way. I will have to admit that I am lost, swallow my pride, and turn into the nearest gas station. I'll assume a jaunty attitude that I don't feel, and I will find a human being to take the place of my maps and guides and technological devices to give me directions. I may have to stop more than once, and it will be late when I get home. I'll get stuck in rush hour traffic, but eventually I will make it.

My friend's parents will not complete their journey alone. I pray that one day they will be able to accept help without feeling shame, without feeling that they have failed if they need companions on their way. I pray that their children will understand and respect them, even in their most diminished state. It takes courage—and a bit of bravado—to travel alone. It may take even more courage—and a big dose of humility—to ask for help.

Lost and found

My purse was stolen! Just writing the words makes my stomach knot.
A friend commiserates, "Your life is in your purse."

It happened in the small suburban office where I had appointments
with my spiritual director and my acupuncturist. I got there early,
read my book in the waiting room, and then got up to go to the
bathroom. Somewhere, between here and there, when there was no
other person around, the purse disappeared. The staff was alerted
and—all hands on deck—we wore a path in the carpet between the
two rooms, scouring them both.

Are you sure you didn't leave it at home?
Yes . . .
Is there anyone there who could check for you?
No . . .
Did you stop any place else?
My local coffee shop, but I called there, and they turned up nothing.
Did you check your car?
Yes. Fortunately, the keys are in my coat pocket.
How long have you been here?
Twenty minutes.
Where do you think you left your purse?
On the floor by my chair or on the shelf in the bathroom.
Did you hang your purse anywhere?
No . . . No . . . No . . . I was so sure . . . and then I wasn't.

There was nothing to do but call 911. A very kind policewoman
arrived promptly. She was polite and efficient, and if she thought
it odd that I would meet her by the front door with needles in my
forehead and my thumb, she didn't mention it. I suppose she knew
I was not an escape risk. We went through the drill. How did it
happen? What was in your purse? How much money? What else?
Cell phone, dark glasses, calendar, credit cards and receipts, blank
check, medical insurance identification, driver's license, family
contacts for an emergency . . .

I finished treatment but the shock wore off when I got home and the mopping up began. First, a deep breath, a sandwich, and a glass of wine, then I was on the phone until late in the night explaining what happened, canceling credit cards and talking to the bank, gratified to learn that many institutions have customer service departments open 24/7.

As soon as they opened in the morning, I called Social Security to report a lost Medicare card. I was told to come to the St. Paul office. So in a late spring blizzard, I finally found a parking spot blocks away, wandered around the city until I reached their office, and walked in to see a waiting room with no fewer than fifty people ahead of me. I stepped to a window.

Can I get a replacement card here?

Oh, no! You have to go to Minneapolis.

But . . . but . . . your website says St. Paul, the woman on the phone told me to go downtown St. Paul.

Sorry! The location just changed.

Can I apply online or by phone or mail?

No, you must go there in person.

I pocketed a slip of paper with the address of the Minneapolis office twenty miles away and resolved to go to Social Security on another day. I planned to get there as soon as the office opened and to bring a book. Maybe I would finally get through *Moby Dick*.

I drove through icy, blocked streets to check off the rest of my list: cash a check, apply for a new driver's license, buy a new cell phone, order glasses . . . This process was exasperating and very expensive! It was a nightmare from which I wouldn't wake up soon.

I know that many, many people have purses lost or stolen. I know it didn't happen to me because I am old. Foolish, yes. Too trusting. Careless. But I have had conversations in person and on the phone with concerned and caring strangers as well as supportive friends and family who genuinely want to help. I have not felt patronized at all. Someday probably I will be, so under all the other emotions—the anger and annoyance and gratitude—there lurks the fear that other people may be wondering if I am losing it, if I am too old to be responsible for my own affairs. Fear attaches itself like a shadow, whispering in my ear, except in those lovely high noon moments when I completely forget myself. I want to have more of those.

Eventually my purse was found—right where I had left it in a dark corner of the coffee shop. My stolen identity was retrieved, and I can be myself again—an older and wiser self, I hope. I have learned that stupid and annoying things can happen at any age, that I am still capable of doing the laborious grunt work of correcting this kind of mistake, that I can laugh about it afterwards, and that I need to laugh and not to judge or blame.

Belonging

In his book *The Memory of Old Jack*, Wendell Berry describes the main character at the end of his life: "He would be faithful to what he belonged to: his own place in the world and his neighborhood, to the handful of men who shared his faith. He had taken his final stand. He would accept no comfort that was not true."

The most challenging task of aging may be to know what is true. To discover where we are, understand where we belong and to whom we belong, and to follow our faith. We spend a lifetime on this voyage of discovery, but when we are young we cannot see the distant shore and we could never believe that when we reach shore at last, our voyage may have circled round to the very harbor from which we set sail.

Elders dwell more and more on the past, dreaming dreams while the young see visions. We search for and befriend our "inner child." We may take delight in remembering youthful exploits and personality traits—especially the ones that got us into trouble. We may even see our strengths there and be proud of how we overcame or channeled that negative energy. We can laugh at ourselves more easily, talk more openly with old friends and family about the memories we share. We learn to have more compassion for others as well as for ourselves—the young people we were and the old folk we have become. We seek truth because there is no time for pretense and no comfort in it and because we still have a lot to learn.

Pondering

It is overwhelming sometimes to realize how much we can gain or lose in a lifetime. It is inspiring how we can learn to adapt.

Pets die; grandparents and older friends do too. Then our parents and the generation ahead of us till we are left standing, bowed but not alone, that is if we are very lucky, if we can participate in the normal order of things. But what are the odds?

In our city ghettos, in the war-torn Middle East, and in the famines of Africa, the chances are great that children will die before their parents, that whole families will be broken or lost. Death may be lurking around every corner, yet men work in the fields and drink coffee in sidewalk cafes and women still go to market. Children go to school and even play games in the street. Many of them grow up to be healthy, responsible citizens.

How is that possible? Their strength is a testimony to the human spirit and a back of the hand to "the slings and arrows of outrageous fortune."

I wince when I hear "God doesn't give you more than you can carry." I don't believe in a God that gives us war and hunger and disease. They are part of the human condition, but joy and sorrow, and failure and success are not individually parceled out nor are they distributed evenly. "It's not fair!" our children cry, and we try to teach them early. No, life is not fair.

We help as we can; we earnestly do what we can but we cannot correct the cosmic imbalance. So here are some of the questions we ask as we age:

How can I make my little life worthy of the space it has taken on the planet and the resources it has consumed?

Have I made a meaningful contribution?

Did I invest my talents or bury them?

How can I carry another's burden?

The questions won't be answered by us but by our children and the generations that follow. Is that fair? It's worth pondering.

What if?

In just over a year my grandson Tyler will graduate from college. He is looking for a summer internship, having job interviews, exploring his alternatives, and asking the big questions. In an environment where jobs are hard to come by, he is surely worrying and wondering, "What will happen if . . . ?"

On the other end of the spectrum, I am asking myself, "What would have happened if . . . ?" What if I had made other choices, taken the roads not traveled? Did I choose as freely as I thought I did?

Sometimes looking back, life seems very arbitrary—a series of lucky or unlucky breaks. At other times I feel that I must have an internal GPS that is constantly recalculating to keep me on the right path. The other day, I reread my Myers-Briggs profile that describes my personality type so accurately that I might have been destined to become who I am and to do what I did, though I could never have predicted making some of the decisions that led me here. ENFJs are teachers, idealists, networkers who articulate, articulate . . .

There were painful times that I wish I could do over or erase: leaving college to marry at nineteen, divorce and a broken family, wounds inflicted on all sides. There were joyful times that I wish could have lasted forever: going back to school, meeting Bob, blending five teenagers and an eight-year old, writing and farming and working in the church—blessings given and received. It was not always easy and certainly not what I expected, but I can't imagine any other life and I am very grateful. When Tyler is my age, I want my grandson to feel grateful too.

There are so many factors out of our control! Accidents, injury, health issues, the extensive family environment, social upheaval, forces of nature. I don't want him to know that yet; he will discover it soon enough. I want him to think he can be master of his universe, to have utmost confidence in his ability to make the good choices he is very capable of making.

He will make mistakes, of course. We all do. But I want him to have the freedom to act as he thinks best. I want him to take risks, to follow his dreams.

I would like both of us to ponder the epitaph of the unknown man in Lakewood Cemetery, Minneapolis, whose headstone reads: The only regrets I have are the temptations I successfully resisted.

Just say NO

When I was a young married woman, a friend of my mother's whom I loved and respected asked me to help her with some committee work of one kind or another—I don't remember what. I had a baby and two toddlers so I muttered, mumbled, nattered on about how busy I was . . . until she kindly cut me off. "Don't apologize, don't explain." I didn't understand then, and I felt burdened if I said yes, guilty if I said no.

I understand now because I am old, and I have earned the right to say no—a clear, resounding NO.

No, I don't go to parties by myself.

No, I won't finish reading this selection for our book club.

No, I won't eat kale (because I don't like it, that's why!).

This new freedom extends to personal relationships as well. In the past I may have stifled them . . . in apology and explanation.

My neighbor and I were estranged for years. I wanted to do something, understand what went wrong, talk about it, and fix it. But reconciliation finally came when I could just let go and let time do the healing. Eventually we put the issues behind us—or we forgot what they were. Older people have trouble remembering the past anyway, and we outwear hurts and grudges. They are leached of toxicity, and we don't feel the need to dig around in the dirt of blame and recrimination. Instead we plant new clean seeds and tend the present. We start where we are and we live for today.

Now I can sit in my neighbor's sunny kitchen, gratefully drinking coffee and sampling her delicious apple kuchen. I feel free to say to her:

YES, I love you.

NO, I won't serve on your committee.

April 25

It is snowing!

Not just a melt-as-it-lands snow, but a stick-around, "winter storm warning" snow. We have had one April blizzard after another, and the forecast is for unseasonably cold weather into next week, which according to my calculations is May.

We Minnesotans are always a little crazy in this season that passes for spring, but never more so than this year. We are desperate for sun and warmth and color. I went to a meeting the other day where there were six women scattered among the men's grey suits, all of us in gaudy, clashing pinks and reds and orange. When a seventh woman entered the room wearing beige, she smiled, "Oh, oh, I didn't get the dress code." But she could be excused; she had spent the winter in Florida.

Last Sunday in church, a man with gallows humor reminded me that in just two months the days would be growing shorter. At the peak of summer then, we probably will have skipped spring altogether. Our worship was somber, as out of season as the weather—more Good Friday gloom than Easter joy. Until this spell passes, it will be hard to have hope and believe in new life.

Many older people have bouts of depression, and this must be a taste of what it is like. Trapped at home day after grey day by the hostile universe of icy roads, blocked sidewalks, and blowing snow, I'm short on supplies, lonely for friends, and afraid to go out. I want to burrow down into my quilt and stay there. But my escape fantasies lead me instead to the computer. On a whim, I google retirement communities in California and Arizona.

Let's see . . . I meet the age requirements . . . I think I could pass the physical exam . . . I know some interesting people who live in this one . . . that one is beautiful—just look at all the gardens . . . I could come back to Minnesota for the summer . . . I'm sure the family would visit.

I print pictures off web pages and prop them in the kitchen. As I putter about, I come to the conclusion that I am not trapped after all. If I wanted to, I could move to a warm climate where my joints would feel better, where I could be more active, and where I could meet new people and maybe learn new skills. I would desperately miss friends and family but nothing and no one is forcing me to live in Minnesota; it's my choice. Crazy as it is, it's my choice. I am old, but still. For as long as I can, I will make my own choices.

The snow has stopped momentarily, though the sky is still full of it. All the branches of trees and bushes are white, the ground looks like a fresh meringue, and traffic is quiet. I look out the kitchen window onto a winter wonderland.

Yes, I have to admit it, I may be crazy, but even in April it's beautiful.

Possessed

I'm sure it never occurred to me when I was a young wife and mother, moving from apartment to starter home to a house large enough for our growing family, that one day the process would be reversed.

Forty years ago when I drove or walked around the grand old neighborhoods in St. Paul I would ogle the brick mansions and the Victorian brownstones. What would it be like, I wondered, to have all that room for children? The high ceilings, leaded windows, polished woodwork. The turrets! The wide front porches!

Later when I came back to the city as a widow with children grown, I wistfully admired cozy Craftsman bungalows in small residential neighborhoods. But I settled in a condo because I did not want to be responsible for the maintenance of house and yard.

In between I lived on a sprawling farm with outbuildings for tools and machines and boxes and boxes of "treasures" that kids outgrew but couldn't bear to part with. Downsizing has been a long, slow process of moving from the farm to a house on the North Shore and back to the city—back to the beginning with the belongings of seven people distilled into space for one.

I feel possessed by possessions! Like most elders who reach this milestone and begin the process, I asked the question: What do I do with all my stuff? Good stuff like antique furniture that is too big for my new small space and china and silverware that I don't need, can't store, and the children don't want to polish. Until recently I had a dozen crystal finger bowls (finger bowls!) that were a generous present for my first marriage. We used them for ice cream but they will have to find another purpose now.

It is hard to part with things we have been given or collected, that we have dusted and cared for and lived among, hardest when they can't be passed down, along with the memories, to someone in the family. It was painful sometimes. Throwing pieces of our family history into the dumpster, setting precious items out on a table to be pawed over and bargained for by strangers, listening to their snide remarks ("Now why do you suppose anyone would want something like this?"), and then going home to the empty space left by Bob's oversized recliner and the large oak table that welcomed our family meals.

I gave away shelves and shelves of books that had warmed our rooms like old friends. I discarded Bob's threadbare lap robe, his pipes and pipe stand; his sons took whatever mementos they wanted—his watch, his hats, his favorite coffee mug. I swallowed hard and threw away their children's artwork. I sorted photographs and albums, but still I have trays and trays of slides for which I would need a screen and projector that I don't own or have room to store; at the back of the coat closet there are shoeboxes of full of glossy 3x5 prints. I feel ungrateful if I don't keep them and burdened if I do.

I have come back to the beginning—starter home to "ender" residence, and sometimes I wonder what all the urgency was about— the determination to build a nest and feather it with beautiful, useful things. It was expensive and time-consuming to gather them, and it is difficult to part with them responsibly. But I am relieved to be settled at last in a smaller space. I feel lighter, more sure of what I own and where it is. I think I made sound decisions most of the time but they were not always rational. I kept a set of my grandmother's dessert plates even though I hardly ever entertain. I saved presents from the children and grandchildren, including a floppy stuffed dog with all the fur loved off of him. And in a special pile on my desk there are books for Dummies to explain the inner workings of the iPad and cell phone for which I will develop new patience and understanding (I will, yes, I will) now that I have entered this new stage and found a new home.

The junk drawer

Almost every kitchen has one—the drawer full of faded, yellowed recipes that we have yet to try, clipped ages ago from magazines and newspapers . . . the brochures from programs long past . . . utensils that don't work well but have a sentimental value . . . manuals for appliances that we may or may not read when something goes wrong . . . Tupperware tops that no longer "burp" . . . rubber bands, bits of string, toothpicks—the catch-all drawer for "miscellaneous."

Years ago my mother helped me move into our blended family's new home. After a long, tiring day of unpacking boxes, wiping shelves, washing dishes, and settling the kitchen, she exclaimed, "Okay, that's it! I will do whatever else you ask of me but I will not unpack any more boxes marked 'miscellaneous!'"

When my friend Cynthia died unexpectedly, she left behind a drawer full of recipes from three generations of women in her family. There were comments written in the margins about the sources and their traditions, old cooking terms were scratched out and updated; over the years ingredients were added, subtracted, and substituted as real butter and heavy cream made way for low-fat, heart-healthy alternatives. What a history/memoir/novel they could compose! Her family may never use the recipes but they can't bear to throw them away.

As we get older, a lot of us resolve to sort out our belongings, to get rid of everything we don't really need, to leave our homes neat and tidy so it will be easy for our heirs. I have fantasies of dying with all my clothes washed and ironed, my desk clear, closets uncluttered, and kitchen sparkling. But when I think back on the kitchens in homes where I've lived, they were happy places. That was where family and friends often gathered—messy and noisy and not sparkling at all.

Pots were often boiling on the stove, flour dusting the counters, and mounds of fruits and vegetables ready to be washed and prepared piled by the sink. But out of those kitchens came soup and bread and jars of preserves, pickles, applesauce, and tomatoes. Birthday cakes were assembled there along with special holiday dishes, old favorite comfort foods, and a few memorable failures. The children tease me still about the zucchini pancakes and my experiment with bouillabaisse and its floating fish eyes.

My father had a workroom in the basement, my husband a shop in the barn. Here were their happy, messy places. Both of the rooms were crammed with unrecognizable parts of machinery and tools, with nuts, bolts, and nails of every size; they were organized by the principle that you keep things "just in case." There was an order not discernible to the feminine eye but woe to the woman who moved any single thing! I'll have to admit that some very clever inventions and repairs were conceived in these spaces where one man's treasure looked, to the uninitiated, an awful lot like trash.

So these memories make me wonder: Do I really want to straighten every closet, sort every drawer? Read every book on my shelves? Pull every weed in the garden? Answer every message in the inbox? If I have checked every item off my to do list, what incentive is there to get up in the morning?

My daughter-in-law gazes longingly into my neat, spare refrigerator. Hers is crammed, as mine once was, with teenage snacks, almost-empty gallons of milk, mysterious leftovers. "I can't wait till mine looks like this," she says. I know how she feels but I know, too, that when the kids are gone she will miss their clutter.

So here is a toast (in a "miscellaneous" glass) to jobs not done and messes not cleaned. Here's to the guarantee that we will be missed, at least for a little while, by the people who step in to do our jobs, finish our terms, sort our belongings, and remove our traces. Here is a hearty thank you to those who will follow. In the very distant future, may they leave behind a happy mess of their own.

Weaver Woman

The old woman is weaving her life together,
strands of joy and sorrow,
a pattern of hope
to wrap around the children.

She weaves as women have always weaved
tending the sick, comforting the broken-hearted,
strengthening the weak . . .

The fabric is almost finished now
and still she mends, she patches and repairs.
There are lumps and loose threads
that escape her fingers
refusing to be entwined.

There is no perfect ending to her story,
no happily ever and ever after,
but as the old woman gathers her life
and folds it into her lap
she sees that the cloth is sturdy, that it shimmers.

8

How do you want to be remembered?

Circle game

When Ali was fifteen, I attended an event at her school. She introduced me to her friends who proclaimed, she told me later, that I was "the most adorable grandmother ever."

A few months and one driver's license later, I became "Granny Who?" When I went to the same event at the school next year, she was nowhere in sight.

I expected this. I remember what I was like when I was sixteen and wanted to spend all my time with friends. I know that she and I have a bond that will never be broken; it will be stretched thin for a few years before it snaps back into a new shape of closeness.

But it happened so fast! Why is it that our grandchildren grow up so much more quickly than our children?

I remember one grey winter day when I was a young mother at home with three children under four—the younger two in diapers, the oldest one with chicken pox. My grandmother, who very seldom dropped by unannounced, decided that day to introduce me to a special friend who was visiting from out of town. The bell rang and there on the doorstep stood two elegant women in fur-trimmed coats with hats and gloves and matching purses. Oh, no!

I was distracted and disheveled to say the least. The kitchen was a mess. The baby was crying as I opened the door. Granny stepped inside and without skipping a beat, she picked him out of the high chair and patted him on the back as he nestled his dirty little face into her coat. "Oh, my dear," she said to me after she had made the introductions, "the time goes so fast!" "Yes," her friend agreed, smiling as she mopped up the counter. "Enjoy it while you can." (I remember shaking my head and wondering if the time would ever go fast enough.)

The dear ladies never took off their coats, and I forgot even to offer them tea but I have never forgotten their kindness or their advice.

When raising young children there are years that are physically demanding. Then there are push me/pull you years that drain us emotionally as children mature and prepare themselves (and their parents) for eventual leave-taking. They can be tumultuous, but looking back even those years seemed to go too fast.

My granddaughter has become a good driver, and she is gaining more and more independence, just at the time when I can anticipate losing my own driver's license and all the freedom it represents. And so the cycle repeats.

The values, the technology, the obstacles, and the opportunities change as one generation replaces another. Time goes faster and ever faster. But my grandmother was right. If I can enjoy every moment of being with those I love, maybe once in a very rare while, I will even be called "adorable."

"What is so rare as a day in June?"

We memorized the verse by James Russell Lowell when we were in school: "Then, if ever, come perfect days."

Today is just such a day. The morning is cool and there is dew on the grass, but the sky is clear, and by midmorning, temperatures will be very warm. As the sun rises, a slight breeze stirs the trees across the street.

When I was a child, I loved mornings like this. I woke early and slipped out of the bedroom I shared with my sisters—very quietly so they wouldn't follow me. In my pajamas and bare feet I ran across wet grass to my favorite tree in our apple orchard. I climbed into my perch about half way up. I leaned my back against the trunk, feeling the rough bark through my flimsy top, stretching my wet legs along a sturdy branch that faced the sun.

Hidden here, in my special private place, I felt safe and clever. Here I watched the shadows fade and listened to the woods wake up, here I read Nancy Drew mysteries, dog stories by Albert Payson Terhune, and *Little Women*. I read until the household woke up. My father drove off to work; the screen door slammed and my sister called me in for breakfast.

As I remember summers when I was young, they are an endless stream of perfect days always spent outside. But I felt rich and free and fearless then; I know my limits now. I know these days are rare.

Today is the summer solstice, and I have come out on my deck at dawn to celebrate, languishing here in my bathrobe on a lounge chair padded with cushions, bare feet stretched toward the sun. There is a book in my lap, and on the table next to me, a cup of strong coffee— my concession to old age. From the third floor I look into the distant tops of trees. The endless rhythm of city traffic beats under the bird songs and the quiet I cherished long ago.

A friend says that living in the city during the summer is like being "a bug in a bottle." In the middle of the day, we have to close our windows and shut deck doors against the noise of sirens and trucks and buses and motorcycles. We glimpse the birds through glass but we don't hear them sing. We see the leaves rustle but we don't feel the breeze.

On my to do list today: Clear The Desk. Capital letters! There are bills to pay, emails to answer, phone calls to return. But one of my prerogatives as a woman is that I can change my mind, and being an older woman I am not so bound by a schedule. I should . . . I must . . . I ought to stay inside. When I was younger, I probably would have. But today I won't.

Today I am going to stay outside. I may have to walk on sidewalks instead of wandering through the grass barefoot, but at least I can walk. I may not have a garden to tend any more or work to do in the out of doors, but I can appreciate the gardens in my neighborhood and all the labor that goes into maintaining them.

I could stroll on the pathways by the river and contemplate the ageless mystery of the Mississippi, take a book and sit on a bench there. I could visit one of the city parks nearby or call a friend to walk with me on Grand Avenue and stop for an ice cream cone at one shop or a latte at another—or even do both!

This is a day to celebrate, to be reckless, to feel young, even as I am aware of all the limits of my age. So . . . it's off with the desk work and on with the sunscreen, the dark glasses, the sturdy orthopedic shoes, and long-sleeved shirt. It's a beautiful day—and I'm going to pull the cork out of the bottle.

Farmer's market

It is early Saturday morning, and I am in the midst of the jostling, good-natured crowd that strolls the aisles of the farmer's market downtown, ogling red mounds of tomatoes, baskets of green beans and lettuce and peas, carrots and beets and peppers in every hue, and gaudy mixed bouquets of fresh flowers.

I feel a tug on the back of my jacket. Turning around I see a little boy looking up at me with big brown eyes and a tentative smile. "Remember me?" he asks. I don't—and before I can stop myself, I admit it. "Galtier," he prompts. That is the school where I volunteer, but I have never been in his classroom. He must be in kindergarten or first grade, younger than the kids I teach.

I hug him, talk a bit with his family, and then watch with tears in my eyes as they melt back into the crowd. Tears because he had the courage to approach me, and I feel I let him down; tears because the school has been redistricted, and he will not go back so I won't see him again; tears because for one brief moment I could believe that I had made a difference in the school simply by being an approachable presence. It was a moment of grace.

It was a stark reminder, too, that wherever we are, whatever we do, we are known. Friends and strangers are watching, yes, and judging, criticizing, admiring . . . who knows? Much as we would like to think that we always make a good impression or that we have no enemies that is very likely not true.

This life is not a dress rehearsal; we are not on stage. In the time I have left I want to discover and to be my most genuine, fallible human self. But at the same time, I think we elders need to recognize that younger people are watching us. We are their mentors and guides through the challenges of aging. They want us to be cheerful, welcoming, and strong. They want to know us at our best, and they want us to know them.

"Remember me?" the little boy asks.

How could I forget?

Tell me a story

I am a little girl sitting at a large table, gathered with my family for a festive meal of some kind—Thanksgiving perhaps or an anniversary celebration. I am all dressed up, squirming on a straight-backed chair in my stiff new dress, dangling feet pinched into shiny patent leather shoes. Under the watchful eyes of stern and proper grown-ups, I sit quietly, not speaking unless I am spoken to (and never with my mouth full), carefully choosing and using the right utensils, folding my napkin in my lap. At the head of the table is the family patriarch, droning on . . . and on . . . telling one story after another . . . stories in which he is always the hero, as if a long life were license to take up all the airspace in the room.

I am a young woman at a large, raucous picnic, meeting the new family I am about to join. Aunts and uncles and cousins and grandparents cluster in small groups, laughing and shouting to one another, sharing their memories about the good old days. They pause politely when I am introduced then turn back to conversations that don't include me.

More and more, memories like these float to the surface. When I am in a mixed age group, I am conscious of how the older people (people who are now my age) tend to monopolize the conversation. Maybe we live alone and appreciate having an audience; maybe we want younger people to understand how things are "supposed to" be; maybe we need assurance that our hard-won wisdom is valuable to others and our lives have meaning. The motives are understandable but the conversations make me squirm as I did many years ago.

I don't want to live in the past. I want us to be present to one another now, and I want my generation to talk with those who are younger about the future that we are creating together. At the same time, it is important to "remember when."

In a few weeks I will go to a mini reunion of college classmates.

We are scattered all over the country, but we have kept in touch, one way or another, for almost sixty years. We share a history and speak the same language. Our gathering will be poignant because we know that we may never be all together again. We will be energized by our meeting, and no one will be left out. But what would our children and grandchildren think if they were plunked down in the middle of our stories? Probably just what I thought when I was young . . . BORING.

It is gratifying when a young person wants to know about the past and takes an interest in preserving family history. We should do all we can to spark that interest, not only with our stories but also with theirs. If we can listen more and talk less, we may be able to understand what our children are really asking. What is important to them? How have we been shaped by the past, and how can they hope to be guided? Like us, they want to know where they came from so they can better understand who they are.

I know very little about my family except cold, hard facts. I would like to know my ancestors better, to know flesh and blood human beings with all their strengths and all their foibles. I want funny stories and sad stories, with a sprinkling of heroes and happily ever afters. Unfortunately all my biological grandparents died before I was born, so I didn't have access to those resources.

I am an old woman. My granddaughter has come for a visit, and we are sitting at the dining room table with scrapbooks spread out and loose pictures in piles around us. She is asking me who these strangers are and what they are doing. She is seeing her father as a young boy and discovering how much her brother looks like him. "Is that you, Grammy?" she asks about the dark-haired farm woman wearing a bandana and blue jeans.

There have been many moves and a painful unraveling of my family since these pictures were taken, and I have not looked at them for many years. But as Ali questions me, the fabric begins to mend. I am finding answers. We are writing a new history, beginning again.

Lasting value

Most of us in our seventies are discovering that kids don't want our "stuff"—the silverware, the gold-rimmed china, the mahogany antiques. They don't want "things" passed down through the generations. They want furnishings from Ikea that can be assembled quickly and then knocked down in a few years to be replaced.

When I have the chance to visit old friends, I often see treasures that were in their parents' home. I recognize a lamp, a chair, or an ashtray (though none of us smoke anymore), and I feel comforted. Old-fashioned? Yes. Impractical? Perhaps. But these items hold memories, as do the books on my shelf that I may not read again but want to keep because they are familiar and well loved.

Our kids don't read books much, at least not hardcover books. They read paperbacks or on tablets. I admire—even envy—their technological skills, and I know I will never catch up to the next generation but still, it makes me sad that they can't slow down, meet us halfway, listen to our stories so they understand why our "stuff" is important.

Maybe every generation grows up thinking that it can invent the world—that new is always good and old is always bad. Certainly I thought so, and I regret now that I didn't listen to my elders or pay attention to their tales of the good old days. When I was young I didn't care about my ancestry or family history, and it is too late now to fill the gaps in my knowledge and then pass it on.

I moved from a farm to a house to a condo, downsizing along the way. It was hard. Deciding what to keep, what to sell, or what to give away and to whom.

We'd like things we have enjoyed to be passed on to those we love. But we cannot control the choices of our children, and, in the end, things are only things—important not for themselves but for their stories. Let us not downsize our stories! I'll hear yours and you can hear mine. Who knows? The children may be listening.

Headstones

Our names are on the headstone:

SIMPSON
Robert — Anne

Bob's full name, his date of birth and date of death—five years ago today.

My name and birth date only. It is always a shock to see it there. A not too subtle reminder of where I can expect to be in ten to fifteen years.

I am in the little country cemetery where we bought lots many years ago. It became a family joke when we discovered that the man in charge of the grounds got tired of mowing around stakes so one day he simply pulled them up. It took quite some time to find the plots again because the township official in charge of the cemetery was usually working in his barn where he didn't have a phone. Bob was delighted with this casual, accepting approach to death. It was good theology. After all, who knows, really, how to stake our "final resting place"?

This piece of land was carved out of the farm fields that surround it on three sides, with acres of corn now in tassel. It is quiet here—a lovely, calming quiet that is in stark contrast to the city noise where I live an hour away. I hear robins and chickadees and squirrels in the woods that border the east and overlook a slow-moving river where we used to go tubing. Occasionally there is the cackle of a pheasant, a dog barking on a distant farm, or, a long way off, the distinctive chug-a-chug of a John Deere tractor. It could be coming from the hay field we left twenty years ago.

Today would be a perfect day to put up hay—hot, clear, dry. I remember the rush to turn and bale the cut hay before it rained. High school boys joined our teenagers—all of them dripping wet, working with shirts stuck to their bodies or thrown aside to expose their bare chests to scratches and bug bites. There was good-natured "macho" competition in a marathon of loading, lifting, and piling the bales as they climbed on them to the top of the stifling barn. I remember the enormous amounts of food they could eat at dinner (noon meal), lunch (afternoon snack), and supper. To cut the dust in their mouths and throats, I made them Hay Time Switchel—a noxious blend of vinegar and spices. As they got older, they inevitably discovered that beer could do that job much better.

My mind wanders further, to lambing season in the basement of that same barn—our most joyful and exhausting time of year. Then to the vegetable garden that was my retreat. No cell phones in our pockets in those days. I could mull things over without interruption and get my aerobic exercise as well when I planted, watered, and weeded on hot summer days.

I feel connected to that life today by memory and by what I am wearing: blue jeans, T-shirt, hiking shoes. It is not my daily city wardrobe, but these are the clothes in which I feel most at home.

I am connected, too, by the quiet. I stare at the headstone and think of the mystery of death and life in whatever form it takes. I feel Bob's presence with me, and I know it lives on in his sons and grandchildren too, in their memories and in some of their talents, looks, and mannerisms. He may pop up again many generations from now when one of his descendants, who never will know his name, sprouts the bushy eyebrows that some ancient Scot (maybe a sheep farmer) bequeathed to Bob. Where did they come from?

The questions have no answers. They waft on the gentle summer breeze. They settle quietly in my heart. Rest in Peace.

Fiftieth reunion

We have come from all over the country. In our class are doctors and CEOs, housewives and teachers, and community activists. There are snowbirds, farmers, urban dwellers, and north woods poets. Our hair may be thinner or many shades lighter and our waistlines may be thicker, but we recognize each other by the graduation pictures on our name tags—and by a laugh or a gesture that in one swipe erases fifty years. We are here to meet each other, to know each other again—and possibly to know ourselves.

In some ways we may seem more different and varied than we did in our homogeneous high school years. Without question our lives have taken turns and led us to places we never could have predicted.

Yet in other ways, we are more alike than we were fifty years ago. None of us have escaped pain and loss. Most of our parents are gone as well as many friends and contemporaries. It is sobering to sit in the chapel for our memorial service and hear the names read aloud of classmates who have died.

Our families may be broken, scattered about the globe or clustered close by. We may have a partner or be widowed, be divorced or single by choice. Whatever our current situation, we probably have more freedom than ever before. We are now responsible to but no longer responsible for the next generation. We have time and space to define who we are and how we want to spend the rest of our lives.

We may be dealing with serious health issues; and if not now, we know we will be in the near future. Among us are recovering alcoholics, cancer survivors, and classmates living with chronic illness. We listen respectfully (and a bit fearfully) to the stories of those who have "been there."

At one time or another all of us have made serious mistakes, and now we are more willing to admit them. A few of our classmates who lost everything in the Great Recession are not ashamed to talk about it with others who seem to be healthy, wealthy, and wise. We are much more open, more at home in our own skin than we were at our tenth reunion or even at the twenty-fifth—when we strutted about, puffed with success, full of plans and pretensions, or diffident and embarrassed, stayed at home. It seems that we can accept ourselves more readily, enjoy each other, and laugh more easily.

We promise that we won't wait five years till the next reunion.

We'll stay in touch.

We really mean it, and maybe this time in spite of busy schedules and long distances we will follow through. We know there won't be many second chances.

Questions

When we are confused or make mistakes, we are taught from an early age to turn over a new leaf, wipe the slate clean, to become a good, right, and perfect person. We join the lines of people waiting for treadmills and elliptical machines grinding away at the Y; we stock up on fruits and vegetables at the grocery store; we grudgingly do good deeds; we determine to give up bad habits and doggedly try to adopt new ones. We will reform ourselves, create a hospitable environment for our loved ones, and be a success at every endeavor.

Hmm . . . maybe instead of trying to be a different creature, we should simply accept who and what we are at this moment. Scared? Face the fears head on. Content? Be grateful. Share the joy. It is contagious. Confused? Sit with the questions.

It is tempting and oh so easy to grab onto answers before we have asked all the questions. We crave certainty. We want to be in control. No one wants to live in the nether world of unknowing and yet . . .

If I look back on the path my carefully plotted life has taken, I see detours and dead ends, twists and turns that I could never have expected. There have been influences completely out of my control. I've had wonderful surprises and some painful ones. I've made good choices, and I have made others that weren't so good.

When we were younger, a lot of us focused on what we lacked. But now that we are older, it is easier to accept who we are, what we have been given. "Too late to change now," we can chuckle. "Like it or not, that's just the way I am." But is that true? I question myself.

It is dark this morning and well below zero. The landscape outside my window is black branches and white snowdrifts. The ground is frozen tight. But this is the necessary fallow season; seeds are resting till they can warm and swell.

I will light a candle.

I will sit with the questions.

The answers will come in due time.

Tell me again

Dementia patients are often treated as if their lives are erased with their memories. If we don't know our own stories, how will we know who we are or how we will be remembered?

I remember how Bob's face would soften and his eyes light up when friends or family members told him his stories, things he had done and said—funny or sad, heroic or very ordinary. I don't know if he understood the stories, but he did understand that his life had meaning to others.

Of course if we can, we want to tell our own stories. In senior communities you hear them told over and over, around the dinner tables, on the porch, or in the living room with visitors—and they are embellished with the telling.

Recently a friend was asked to speak to residents of a senior apartment complex. After his talk he stayed around to visit, and they thanked him profusely. "Please come back . . . We need outsiders to talk to!" In other words, like all of us, they want an attentive audience and need someone to hear their stories, to affirm who they were—and who they are.

Sometimes it is taxing to hear the same old, same old stories over and over again. But the storytellers are doing important work. An early-stage dementia patient tells his daughter that he is "dismantled." She understands that he is trying to put himself back together again. As he does that, even as he seeks assurance that his self will somehow be gathered up and live on, he is also weaving together strands of the tradition and the community and the family to which he belongs. His story is their story, our story—both personal and universal. We had better listen up!

There was a plaque in Bob's nursing home that said: A friend knows the song in your heart and sings it back to you when memory fails.

Ava Dale

The Lord speaks through Moses (Deut. 30:19 NIV): "This day . . . I have
set before you life and death . . . choose life." But my friend Ava Dale
is choosing death. A devout Quaker, former missionary, elementary
teacher, and Christian educator, she is one of the strongest, most
disciplined, gentle women I know—following her light, shining it
abroad, giving of herself, and forgiving of others. A determined, loving
peacemaker.

Another bad fall put her into a transitional care unit with a broken
pelvis. She falls often and has already recovered from a broken hip, a
fractured arm, and a multitude of sprains and bruises. She has had
surgery for breast cancer. She is eighty-eight years old and worries
about her "senior moments," anticipating with dread the onset of
dementia. She looks ahead to a bleak future in an institution, her
limited resources dwindling.

After long and prayerful deliberation, she has chosen to go home
to die. She is refusing food and water; hospice has been called in and
measures are agreed upon to ensure that she will feel no pain. Her
large family is gathering to keep vigil with her; it is a very difficult
time for them. Some of the children and grandchildren think she is
noble, others feel that she is committing a mortal sin, and all of them
mourn the loss of their beloved matriarch.

A granddaughter asks, "Grandma, why are you dying?"

Because I AM.

"But why now?"

Because I CAN.

Ava Dale is at peace. The dying process will probably take about
three weeks but after eight days her bright blue eyes are still clear,
her contagious smile cheers her downcast visitors, and she is still as
alert and curious and caring as ever she has been. "I have lived long
enough," she says, deeply grateful for her long life, complete with
all its struggles and grace. "I have been blessed. I've done the best I
could and now, though there are other things I'd like to be able to do,
it is time to let younger people try to set the world straight." She is

convinced that she has lived her allotted span, and she is ready to pass on her blessing.

She hopes that there will be time for understanding and acceptance within her family. She knows, they know, that these days are holy and life changing.

The house is kept as quiet and peaceful as possible. If there is conflict or disagreement, it is settled outside as the children wait on her—patient, protective. Friends are scheduled for short visits, widely spaced. They come to say good-bye and share memories and to tell her what she has meant to them. She feels surrounded by love now, basking in it as she listens to her own eulogies.

"We laughed, didn't we?" she asks me. "We had a good time!" Oh, yes, Ava Dale, you knew how to celebrate the simplest, ordinary moments. You and your large family filled holidays with homegrown music and dancing, did things to peanut butter and jelly that turned picnics into portable banquets. You taught us all to see beauty and to ask questions that you always answered thoughtfully.

We did have a good time! The sadness I feel now is not for her but for those of us who are losing her friendship and her love. For the empty space she will leave behind.

But Ava Dale hears and heeds a call to move on to another place. She is choosing death so that she may affirm life, interpreting Moses so that you and your descendants may live. Not many of us will have her opportunity to choose or the courage to take it. I do not know whether I would want such a death for myself, but it is certainly worth considering deeply. Ever the teacher, Ava Dale is showing us another— and perhaps a better—way.

I rejoice that she can die as she chooses—at home, without tubes and machines keeping her alive, surrounded by loved ones. As she determined how to live her life, now she is dying her death, and whether we approve of it or not, we must honor her choice, release her, and with our blessing, let her go.

The coffee shop

I am sitting on a stool in the nook of a sunny window on a blustery fall Sunday, newspapers spread out on the table in front of me as I sip my latte. There are three dignified, well-dressed people at the next table who appear to be old friends. They are comfortable together, sharing stories and laughing . . . at their parents.

Their elders don't understand about investments any more, they have become too reckless or too conservative, they don't budget their resources wisely, and they don't do what the children tell them. Apparently one father invests his money in tractors for the farm he no longer works. A mother wants to travel but that's ridiculous—her daughter knows she can't afford it, and, besides, she is way too old. Their parents are confused, out of touch, not on top of things. What is to be done?

Well first of all, take away the car keys and the checkbook. Then find a nice safe place where the parents can grow old and die because it is not safe for them to remain in their home. It would be so much simpler if they lived nearby and could be monitored at the children's convenience!

One woman just moved her parents from the small Texas town where they have lived for more than fifty years. Now, she sighs with relief, she will be able to watch over them. I imagine Mom and Dad adjusting to a new community where they have no friends. They must find a social group, a church, new doctors (no easy task in this era when many won't take new Medicare patients), and stores where they can get needed groceries and services and supplies. They must learn to navigate public transportation so they can get around a big, unfamiliar city, and they must acclimatize to winter's snow and cold. All this while being very careful not to burden the children and grandchildren who may be delighted to have them nearby but who, by the way, have their own very busy lives and are not available at a moment's notice.

These three people are not complaining about their parents; their concern seems genuine and the laughter is good-natured. But it is laughter and it is directed at their parents—as complaints may be one day. I can't help but feel apprehensive. What do my children say about me? Are they hatching plans? Laughing behind my back?

I take my half-full coffee cup and clamber down from my perch. I'll leave the papers on the table and find a place to finish my latte on a bench outside, out of the wind. I'll watch the somber grey river flow by, then I'll go for a long quiet walk.

From generation to generation

How long do we support our children . . . adult children that is, forty- or fifty-year-olds? It is a question that would have seemed preposterous until now.

But I know middle-aged people who are in real trouble, through no fault of their own. They have lost their jobs or their houses; they may have serious medical issues not covered by insurance, and they are too young for Medicare. Then there are others who are approaching retirement unprepared. They haven't saved for their children's education and sometimes are still in debt for their own.

It is a wrenching turnabout. Some of my contemporaries are sacrificing their own resources and their sense of security to care for their grown children's needs. It is our job, it is our habit, it is the right thing to do to invest in those who will follow us. So if we have the luxury of choice, that is the investment we make. But it makes us vulnerable to financial setbacks and recession; it also raises the question of whether we are enabling our children to escape consequences of their choices.

Most of the people I know, of all ages, are genuinely concerned about the widening financial gap between young and old and about the burdens this generation is placing on the next. I was shocked when I read an article in *Newsweek* (July 2 & 9, 2012) called "Get the OLD off the ROAD." David Frum warns, "If we don't push back, they'll steal our benefits and bankrupt the country . . . we seem today to hear a new bitterness in the attitudes of the old, a special glee in reproaching and denouncing the young."

I have heard grumbling about "this younger generation," of course. What's new? Our parents and grandparents grumbled about us too . . . so it has been, is now, and so it ever shall be. And I have seen senior protesters with their signs "Hands Off My Medicare," but I have not personally encountered this new kind of bitterness. If it is true that the number of Americans over sixty-five will double by the year 2050, we must be concerned—all of us! As Frum says, "If it is uncaring for society to neglect the old, it's outright suicidal to cannibalize the life chances of the rising generation."

A society that spends more for end-of-life care than for childhood education is, indeed, suicidal. But do we have to take sides? Pit one generation against another? The questions seem urgent, the answers elusive.

Please, can we talk? Calmly and compassionately, let us try to find common ground and work together for the common good—in our families, our communities, and in the wider world.

Reading the obits

In the morning I pour a cup of coffee, read the front page of the newspaper, then turn to the obituaries. "Why do you do that?" my grandchildren ask, as I once asked my grandmother. "To see if I'm still here," she'd wink.

Death is a steady companion now. I have a daily curiosity about whether I have lost another friend or acquaintance and about how old people were when they died (and how many of them were younger than I). It sounds depressing, but strangely enough, it is not.

Maybe I am gathering threads, wanting to know what held other lives together. More and more I see our lives as a whole book of individual chapters, each with a beginning, middle, and end, an anthology of birth and death.

When we are young, we lose pets or grandparents, meet people who are disabled by injuries and disease, or hear about soldiers who don't return from war. We tend gardens as they sprout and blossom and fade in season. And yet we try to remain detached about our own life cycle. As Woody Allen has said, "I don't mind dying, I just don't want to be there when it happens."

And yet, I can't help but wonder how it will happen, when I will die.

After a "courageous battle"—a lingering illness?

Unexpectedly?

Peacefully . . . surrounded by loving family?

I was afraid of death when I was younger. I wanted to have some control over it, as if I could choose the time and place and means. But we have no more control over how we die than we do over what people will say about us afterwards.

I would like to know that I will be missed. I would like a glowing obituary, praising my innumerable contributions to humanity, my heroic efforts to change the world, and my remarkable talents. Wouldn't we all?

But we can't even know who will write our obituary or how that person will be feeling at the time. Maybe she felt sick or had a sleepless night . . . maybe he or she was pressed to meet a deadline.

What we can know is that someday there will be a short notice in the newspaper, along with many other notices about ordinary people, and death—the great equalizer—will have written the last word.

Always the last word. So I might as well relax, pour another cup of coffee, and share the rest of the paper with my grandchildren.

Come to Me

Life crooks her finger,
beckons to me . . . come.

Come out of the shadows
wrap the waning light around your shoulders
turn your face to the sun.
wWelcome your memories one by one,
see how time washes away sorrow
leaving bright, rough nuggets of hope.

Put them in your pockets,
follow me.

There are places to see
and people to love
and there is not much time.

Come.

9

What do you hope you can live to see?

Comfort zone

"Go where you will grow!" he says. We are sitting at the restaurant on my favorite outdoor patio to celebrate. John, our longtime friend who was the Lutheran pastor in tiny Grand Marais, has just been called to the largest church of his denomination in the entire country. I want to rejoice with him (and maybe to assure myself that he is still the bright and funny and unassuming man I've known for twenty years).

"I started my ministry as a chaplain in a nursing home, and I thought I would never want anything more," he says, dazed at the changes in his life. "Always, my goal has been to learn! That means staying on the edge, just out of my comfort zone. Unfortunately, it means always being slightly uncomfortable."

John didn't go looking for opportunities, but because he was open and receptive, they came to him. First the call to the North Shore. "I had always wanted to live there!" We retired to Grand Marais about the time his young family arrived, and their presence was a blessing

in our lives. By coincidence—or holy serendipity—Bob had had his
first pastorate there too. Experienced and wise, always willing to
listen, Bob became John's mentor. They laughed together, walking
and talking on the beach, stopping for a latte at the Java Moose or
drinking the mind-altering Lutheran coffee at the church. Later when
he was diagnosed with Alzheimer's, the tables gradually turned and
John became mentor to Bob.

The next church John served was a midsize congregation in the
very Minneapolis suburb where Bob had gone after he left Grand
Marais. We laughed at the coincidence but we were grateful for it
because eventually Bob had to be placed in a care facility and we,
too, moved to the Twin Cities to be closer to family. John visited
him regularly, and one day when Bob seldom spoke and he had not
recognized friends or family for a very long time, John walked into
his room booming, "Hi, Bob!" in his most cheerful voice. Bob opened
his eyes, smiled so broadly that it made me tear up, and very clearly
responded, "Well . . . I'll be darned!!"

Soon after that John moved to a larger church and had a very
packed calendar, but he ministered to Bob until the end and then
conducted his funeral. Now he has become my mentor too.

"What's going on in your life?" he asks me. I tell him about the
work I do for families living with dementia, the curriculum I wrote
for churches, the surprise of discovering that I like to lead workshops.
"What else surprises you?" I tell him I've been traveling a bit. "Oh,
good! You haven't been able to do that for many years." And . . . believe
it or not, I tell him I have a special companion. "I'm not surprised!" he
exclaims. Well, I am. This was never on my radar screen. "What else?"
I tell him I'm surprised to feel healthy again. Even though I have some
serious medical issues, I do not have as much pain and have more
energy. Maybe it's new medication, maybe the warm temperatures of
summer, maybe a special diet or different exercises or maybe . . . "this
new man in your life?" I don't know but I confess that I am moving out
of my comfort zone.

"You were a wonderful caregiver," says John, "and a loyal wife. No
one could do it better. But that is past. You have a future. Go for it!"

But I'm too old to think about a future . . .

"Why?" he asks.

It may be time to pull in . . .

Again, "Why?"

I've had a good life. I'm thankful for the past.

"So?"

It's foolish to take risks at this age . . .

"You still have a lot to learn!"

John likes his job. He has liked all his jobs. When he was approached to apply for this new position, he resisted. "You don't understand . . . this isn't me . . . " But his reputation as leader and teacher and pastor preceded him and the committee persisted. Another opportunity to learn and grow presented itself and he felt called to accept. "Don't think of all the obstacles," John tells me. "You will worry so much about the future that you can't enjoy the present."

This lunch was my treat, in many ways. When I pay the bill I feel a reassuring calm, the gentle shove into a busy, joyful future—however long that might be. John is showing me the path by example, taking a few steps ahead, looking back over his shoulder, and giving me advice and encouragement I didn't know I needed. As we leave the patio, he gives me a big hug. "Remember," he says, "It's okay to be uncomfortable."

Take a risk

A neighbor in her eighties has double pneumonia. The doctor wants to put her in the hospital. But her family plans a reunion at their cabin on a remote island in Canada. I try to console her . . . tell her how sorry I am that she will miss it.

"Miss it?" She's incredulous. "But of course I'll go!"

On Wednesday a friend from Grand Rapids has six-hour surgery in the Twin Cities for a malignant tumor on her spine. She has rods in her back, is in a body cast, and she needs total care. But her fiftieth wedding anniversary is on Sunday. A party has been planned for months. She wants to go home! So three days after the surgery, against all advice of the specialists, she is in a medi-van on her determined way to Grand Rapids where she will recover in a nursing facility. Friends and family can visit her there, and she will join the party through the marvels of modern technology, talking to guests and viewing them on an iPad.

Are these foolish decisions? Maybe . . .

Are they the right thing to do? Absolutely! The patient is doing what she wants so badly to do.

Family gatherings and visits with friends are the bright lights in an older person's calendar. But always they cast a shadow. Always we wonder . . . will this be the last time? And so we ask ourselves how we want to spend the time we have left and what risks we are willing to take.

No one should make these decisions for us. We need whatever control we can maintain over our own lives. And if we want to take a risk, more power to us! Wish us well and let us go. Sometimes the last time is the best.

Letting go

It may be the last and most difficult task of old age, but it surprises me to realize that it is not the past we must let go—it is the future. The past is imbedded in our hearts and our minds; it clings to our bones. We may reinterpret, reconfigure, and come to new understandings and acceptance, but we do not, we cannot let it go. It is who we are.

The future, however, is our hopes and plans and dreams for who we will be, and they must be held lightly. The great shock (and sadness) of old age is how very little future we have left . . . and how little control we have over it. We may never see our grandchildren grow up, we may not finish a project in which we have invested a great deal of time and energy, and we may not live in the place we call home, surrounded by people we love.

No longer can we make long-range plans. We don't buy things because a salesperson tells us they will last forever or they have a lifetime guarantee. We don't buy green bananas. Sometimes, like Li'l Abner's Joe Btfsplk, we wander around with a little black cloud over our heads, wondering: How long?

We learn not to put off phone calls and visits to friends because we don't know how long we will be able to drive or whether we might see them again. The "ever after" that we believed in, when we were young, shrinks to next year, tomorrow, or this day. Our right/wrong and black/white certainties evolve into tentative choices, the best we can do in a given circumstance. The horizon is in sight, and even if we have had a long life, it seems too short. Over and over again we exclaim, "It went so fast!"

Each age has its own tasks, and we begin to understand that old age challenges us to do the only thing we can do: accept the sadness, embrace the joy, and be grateful for all of it—the crazy journey we call life. We'll moan and squeal and laugh and hang on for a bumpy ride, then when the time comes, we will let it go.

Tight squeeze

He is a lifelong friend. His wife was my sailing buddy and a college classmate. She died four years ago and still he is in the last throes of settling her estate, selling their beloved family lake cabin, and considering where he will grow old. Will he stay in the small town where they lived for thirty years—a community where he feels safe, where he is well-known, and has a role and contributions yet to make? Will he move to the Twin Cities four hours away, where he grew up and where he would be closer to family?

I have been a widow for five years. I have established my own daily rhythms, patterns of work and rest and social stimulation. I had never lived alone before, and I have learned to enjoy my new freedom and my solitude. I get lonely of course (loneliness is the "mostly companion" of old age), and I ache for the days when Bob and I lived together, so close that we had the best of both worlds: we were together when apart and separate when together. I cherish those years and am deeply grateful for them. But I cannot bring them back.

This week I tagged along on a trip to Washington, DC, with some of my friend's college classmates and their wives. I'm sure that I was invited so he would not be the only single person in a group of couples. I don't travel much because I, too, am uncomfortable in that position. But he is good company so I was glad to go. We have had a lovely, a busy time sight-seeing, catching up on news of classmates, discussing the good old college days, and inevitably speculating about the world our children and grandchildren will inherit.

Now the group has disbursed and we are alone, sitting on a bench in the little park across the street from our hotel, basking in the warmth of spring sunshine, enjoying the beauty of the blossoming forsythia and cherry trees. Our friendship is deepening; we are very comfortable together. I really like this man. I want to spend time with him—much more time. But he is eighty-two and I am eighty. Realistically, how much time could we have?

"I'm almost ready to move on," he says, gently taking my cold and winter-weary hand in his. I hold it close . . .with affection and gratitude and confusion and fear.

Could I move on? Would it be disloyal to Bob?

Could I open myself to a new relationship at this advanced age?

Does "moving on" mean moving out of this lovely condo? Or does it mean that he would move into space where my pictures hang on the wall, my clothes hang in the closets, and my own peculiar piles clutter the desk? Would I be willing to share my home with him (or anybody else) or he with me? I am a neatnik. Could we adjust to each other's housekeeping habits? They are deeply ingrained by now, not likely to change.

Could we each adapt to the other's schedule without losing contact with our individual friends and families and special interests?

Health concerns are front and center for all of us now. I do not want to become a full-time caregiver again, or worse, become a burden to be cared for.

Whatever we decide, we will take a leap of faith.

What if we dare to risk?

What if we don't?

In a little while, we will leave the park and board a train to visit friends in Virginia. As we drive to their home from the station, we will pass through the tiny town of Tightsqueeze where there is a rickety narrow bridge over the river that divides the town in two. I feel as though I were standing on that bridge now, near the north bank that is fragrant with thaw, dark and cool. Scattered patches of snow. Flowers may bloom in sun on the other side . . . or weeds.

I clasp his warm and steady hand. A tight squeeze.

Epilogue

The paradox of aging

Old age is not what I expected. Florida Scott-Maxwell writes in
The Measure of My Days, "I grow more intense as I age." I suppose
that most of us who reach our seventies and eighties are surprised
to discover what an active time it is. And yet, why should we not
be intense? We have a lot of work to do in this last stage of our life.
Now is our chance to patch together all the ragged pieces of the past,
creating a quilt of our life so that we might see it whole and so that
it might comfort the next generation.

But it's not easy! Old age is a time of paradox. It is a time of
testing our limits and learning to accept them. A time of retiring
from a job and finding meaningful work. A time of accepting help and
demanding independence. It is wanting to make a contribution and
leave a legacy and knowing, finally, that we will not determine how
we are remembered.

Now is our time to offer forgiveness and to seek it, if we can—
even as we realize there may be issues that will not be resolved in
our lifetime. Not all of us will be able to use this bonus time. We may
be impaired physically, mentally, or emotionally. So if we are lucky,
this is a stage of life that we should take very seriously.

And yet, more than ever, we want to play. We laugh at ourselves; we break the rules. We learn to give up control. As we did when we were young, we can savor a beautiful day and appreciate the natural world without feeling any need to tame it. We can give our undivided attention to children and simply have fun together without feeling responsible for their discipline, letting imagination run wild as we teach and learn.

We may unearth interests and talents buried long ago, or we may break fresh ground and commit ourselves to learning new skills without being afraid to make mistakes. We plan social outings and yet we become comfortable with solitude. When we are lonely, we learn to reach out to others who are isolated.

The changes come fast . . . and faster. We may have to move from our home, our neighborhood. We lose health and strength and dreams. We grieve friends and family. But gradually we discover that grief embraced can be transformed into gratitude.

As the body and mind fall away, the spirit burns clean—bright sparks of all that we have been flare up into the self we are.

As we come to the end of our life cycle, we know that death lies ahead and rebirth in a form we cannot fathom.

But we are alive NOW. We have this moment and only this moment. In old age we realize that this is all we ever had.

Acknowledgments

I am grateful to Sam King and Karen Hering who encouraged me to write and supported this project, to my readers Joan Johnson and Abby Dawkins, to my poets' group in Duluth, and to the memoir writers at Macalester Plymouth Church in St. Paul.

I have been blessed by friends and contemporaries who are willing to share their stories, and by Lyndall Johnson who teaches me to embrace aging.

Thank you to my publisher Bill Huff and editor Susan Niemi—you are a delight to work with.

I could not have finished this manuscript without Tanya Spishak and her calm demeanor—giving tech support, answering endless questions, even bringing me more memory (don't I wish!).

Thanks to my generous companion Todd Driscoll who was willing to do the illustrations in exchange for a home-cooked meal, though he knows I'm not a very fancy cook.

Above all, a heartfelt thanks to my granddaughter Alison Leslie, her brothers Tyler and Evan, and the loving family who let me share their lives and feel privileged to grow old.